THE INVESTOR'S GUIDE TO

SHORT-TERM
TRADING
AND
LONG-TERM
INVESTING

THE INVESTOR'S GUIDE TO

SHORT-TERM
TRADING
AND
LONG-TERM
INVESTING

Winning strategies for trading profits *and* capital growth

CHARLES VINTCENT

FINANCIAL TIMES

Prentice Hall

An imprint of Pearson Education

London · New York · San Francisco · Toronto · Sydney · Tokyo · Singapore
Hong Kong · Cape Town · Madrid · Paris · Milan · Munich · Amsterdam

PEARSON EDUCATION LIMITED

Head Office:
Edinburgh Gate
Harlow
Essex CM20 2JE
England

London Office:
128 Long Acre
London WC2E 9AN
Tel: +44 (0)20 7447 2000
Fax: +44 (0)20 7836 4286

Website: www.business-minds.com

First published in Great Britain 1997

The right of Charles Vintcent to be identified as author
of this work has been asserted by him in accordance with
the Copyright, Designs and Patents Act 1988.

ISBN 0 273 63057 1

British Library Cataloguing in Publication Data
A CIP catalogue record for this book can be obtained from
the British Library.

5 7 9 10 8 6 4

Typeset by Northern Phototypesetting Co Ltd, Bolton
Printed and bound in Great Britain by
Biddles Ltd, Guildford and King's Lynn

*The Publishers' policy is to use paper manufactured
from sustainable forests.*

FOREWORD

By Lord Rees-Mogg

More and more people are learning to invest their own money. Some do so in order to avoid paying the charges made by institutional investors which normally come to a significant proportion of the dividend income. Some have realised that institutional investors have to deal in very large quantities of stock, and cannot take advantage of small local companies which sometimes provide the best investments. Some do it because it interests them – following their shares has been a profitable use of time in retirement.

Charles Vintcent, who has a lifetime's experience of stock-markets, has written an excellent introductory work. It not only tells people how to make use of the information they will need, but also gives them very sound advice on short- and long-term investment strategies. It will be of value to all investors, experienced or not, but for the relatively inexperienced it will save them years of learning time and perhaps some nasty shocks on the way.

This is a very sensible and well informed book and I think that the smaller investors who follow it – not all of whom are very small – will find that it helps them both to avoid losses and to make profits. Above all, it will help them to understand what they are doing and how to increase their chances of investment success.

William Rees-Mogg

For Wendy

ABOUT THE AUTHOR

Charles Vintcent is associated with the firm of Keith, Bayley, Rogers & Co., members of the London Stock Exchange. He has been a stockbroker for seventeen years and specialises in advising private clients. He was educated at Charterhouse and has been working in the City since 1960 with the Charterhouse Group and Hambros Bank.

In addition to writing articles for various magazines, his first book about investing on the Stock Exchange, *Be Your Own Stockbroker* was written for those who are newcomers to the world of stocks and shares. This book is its sequel. He gives lectures regularly to private investors who want to know more about ways to invest successfully without having to spend a great deal of time on research. He can be contacted at Keith, Bayley, Rogers & Co., 93–95 Borough High Street, London SE1 1NL, Telephone 0171 378 0657.

CONTENTS

PART 2: INVESTING

ACKNOWLEDGEMENTS

I should like to thank John Arter of Old Mutual International Limited for his invaluable help and advice and also Bill Hubard for explaining the intricacies of spread betting. I acknowledge the debt I owe to Lord Rees-Mogg for taking the time and trouble to write the foreword and to Howard Saunders for the gratuitous supply of all those megabytes.

INTRODUCTION

Everyone who invests in shares does so with the object of making money. Some are more successful than others. This book explains how to manage your own investments so that you get above average performance.

As a stockbroker, I know that the vast majority of those who have money to invest want to combine two different elements in their objectives. They want safety as well as quick profits. **This book will show you how to get both.**

It will show you how to find the shares which are suitable for your long-term investment objectives, as well as explaining how to find the shares which will give you a quick profit for your short-term trading.

There is no difficulty in finding the shares. Information technology (IT) has advanced to such a degree, and is improving by leaps and bounds all the time, so that you can find all the data you need without having to spend hours of tedious work compiling records and analysing them before you choose which to buy and when to sell. This book describes in detail how to use the tools which are readily available so that you can compete on equal terms with the professionals.

To be successful you need to be able to adopt totally different and separate philosophies and disciplines for short-term trading and long-term investing.

This book will show you what is required in your approach to both. It will enable you to equip yourself with the essential knowledge to maximise your profits and set achievable targets for growth and it will demonstrate how to use IT to save you hours of time and help you to pick winners.

In the 1960s, there was a man called Bernard Cornfeld who formed an investment company called 'Investors Overseas Services'. When he interviewed salesmen who wanted to work in the business, he asked them one question only: 'Do you **sincerely** want to be rich?'

Not all his salesmen became rich, but quite a few of them did. I mention this because two important ingredients in successful investing are:

- the real and continuing desire to make money, and
- the ability to concentrate on the right approach to the different investment tactics.

This book is divided into two parts. The first explains what is required for short-term trading, and the second describes how to be a long-term investor. You will find that short-term trading can be addictive and give you a great deal of satisfaction. It can be great fun too. You will lose some and you will win some – the trick is to win more times than you lose. This book will show you how to do it.

PART

1

TRADING

INTRODUCTION TO PART 1

In my book *Be Your Own Stockbroker*, I explained what it is that the different types of shares are designed for. I described the various influences which affect the prices of these different shares and why some are more responsive to raising or lowering interest rates than others. In addition, I demonstrated what an investor could reasonably expect to see by way of growth in the price of an ordinary share compared to that of a gilt in the normal course of events.

The purpose of this book is to show you how to put those lessons into practice and how to make the greatest profits from managing your own portfolio. To do this effectively, you need to separate your investment activities into two separate compartments – **short-term and long-term.** You will have to learn two completely different approaches to the way you think about each investment and be prepared to adopt totally opposing philosophies for each type of operation.

Short-term trading

The Press gives a great deal of coverage to the huge profits (and losses) made by international currency speculators – millions of pounds of profit arising from buying or selling short sterling, the US dollar, the D-mark or the yen. This book is not concerned with such trading since you need to have a great deal of capital to play in that league.

We *are* concerned with the average investor whose resources are limited and who would like to make regular short-term profits, however small relatively, and who wants some of the excitement inherent in trading shares regularly over short periods.

WHAT IS
MEANT BY
SHORT-TERM
TRADING?

INTRODUCTION

In this chapter we describe:

- the definition of 'short-term trading'
- what mental attitude is needed to be a trader and what disciplines you should follow
- what controls are required to trade successfully
- what equipment you need
- how to decide which way you find investment opportunities
- how to forecast price movements using Fibonacci fan lines
- spread betting.

QUESTIONS PEOPLE ASK ABOUT SHORT-TERM TRADING

The best way to start is with a number of questions which I am asked frequently and whose answers will cover all the salient points for you.

How short is 'short-term'?

There are some people who deal on the London Stock Exchange regularly to whom 'short-term' means buying in the morning and selling at a profit the same day! If it were possible to do that five days a week and then we all would be millionaires. However, having said that, there are people who make a comfortable living out of spread betting (see below) doing just that. They may not become millionaires but all their gains are tax free.

> 'The best way to start is with a number of questions which I am asked frequently.'

In the past the chance of making considerable sums of money from short-term trading in the market was available only to those privileged few who worked in the market – and the reason was quite simple. They had access to the prices of all the shares at all times during market hours. Now, with the availability of 'real time' prices via PCs and the Internet, many more people can enjoy these same advantages – impossible until a few months ago. In fact, you *can* buy in the morning and sell the same day and make a profit if you deal in traded options, but this is a very dangerous game and requires constant supervision of your PC screen with real-time prices being downloaded to your computer. The average private investor does not want to spend all day in front of a PC.

Nevertheless, it is not often that a share price moves up sufficiently within one day's trading period for the average trader who is not in the market to rely on making good profits every day and do so consistently throughout the year. So it is more realistic to set a time limit for short-term trading which is more likely to be fruitful under normal market conditions. For the purpose of this book when we ask the question 'How short is short-term?' we mean three to six months.

What are we trying to achieve by short-term trading?

The objective is quite simple. It is to make sufficient profit each time we trade to make the exercise worthwhile and to do so often enough to get an above-average return on the capital employed, net of all dealing costs, so that the effort and time spent in managing the investments is justified. Unless the stockmarket is falling out of bed, it is perfectly possible to achieve such an objective without spending more than 30 minutes a day and at the same time to get a lot of fun and satisfaction out of the exercise.

Let us look at a simple example.

■ EXAMPLE

Say the price of a share on 3 January is 100p to buy and you invest £2,000. You buy 2,000 shares. (For the purpose of this illustration we shall ignore dealing costs and government stamp duty. A more detailed example is given later on in this book).

If the share price rises sufficiently for you to sell them for 110p before the end of March, you will have made 10 per cent profit on your capital.

2,000 shares × 10p = £200 gain.

You have achieved this within three months, and if you did this four times a year you would have made a capital gain of £800 on your stake of £2,000. *You would have made a very respectable return on your capital of 40 per cent.*

Under current tax legislation, you can make capital gains of up to £6,500 per annum completely free of tax *per person*. Thus the concession allows a husband and wife to accumulate £13,000 of gain between them each year without any liability to tax whatsoever.

This objective is simple to state, but is it easy to reach?

Until recently, for the ordinary investor outside the stockmarket, the answer would have been 'no'. However with the investment technology which is now available to everyone for relatively little cost, you can play the game just as effectively as the professional traders in the Stock Exchange. But just going out and buying a computer will not by itself turn on the profits tap. You should not be under any illusion that there is a magic wand which will make you rich if you simply wave it in a certain direction. It does require some knowledge of how the stockmarket works, what makes share prices move and how to read the signals which are there for all to see. The beauty of modern computer technology is that it will take all the hard work and drudgery out of the essential research and record-keeping, which is a vital part of the range of tools which you will need to be successful and make profits consistently.

Everyone who has any experience of investing on the stockmarket knows that share prices do not move up or down in convenient straight lines. Their normal behaviour is to move erratically in a series of zigzags, even when the market as a whole is following a clearly defined trend. Nevertheless, it is perfectly possible to make small but regular profits if you stick to the rules which govern trading and get your timing right when you buy. The difficult thing to achieve is to forecast exactly when the share price will reach the level required to give you your target profit, and it may take slightly longer than you have anticipated.

However, more of this later on in the book when we describe in detail how to control the risks and reduce the unknown quantities to the minimum.

The most important tool for a trader is the chart showing the share price history over the recent past. Because charts occupy such a critical position in decision-making, we shall devote a considerable amount of Part 1 of the book to describing how to read them and the signals which they give, both as to when to buy and when to sell among others. Nevertheless it is useful to introduce them to you gradually. Figures 1.1 and 1.2 show the charts of just two shares covering the period mid-February 1996 to mid-February 1997. Figure 1.1 is the chart of Tate & Lyle and Figure 1.2 is the chart of British Telecom. There are many other shares whose charts present similar pictures of historic price movements.

You will see from both charts that the fluctuation in share price over the period of 52 weeks was such that you could have bought and sold the shares several times and made at least 5 per cent net profit each time within the year. Later on in this book we shall examine the ways in which you can put the information which is contained in the charts to the best practical use. You should look for companies whose share price record shows constantly volatile behaviour because the chances are that the pattern will be repeated in the future.

If I am to trade successfully, do I have to spend all day glued to my PC or the television?

The short answer to that is no. With modern technology you need spend no more than 30 minutes a day monitoring the progress of your portfolio. However, there may be occasions when you are anticipating a jump in the price for specific reasons. For example, you may have read or heard that there could be a bid for the company in the offing, or, the company is due to announce its results and you believe

Fig 1.1 Tate & Lyle: historic price movements mid-February 1996 to mid-February 1997

(Source: Topic)

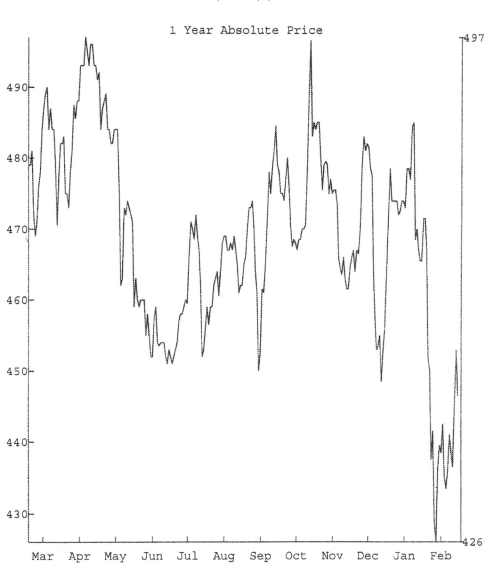

Fig 1.2 British Telecom: historic price movements mid-February 1996 to mid-February 1997

(Source: Topic)

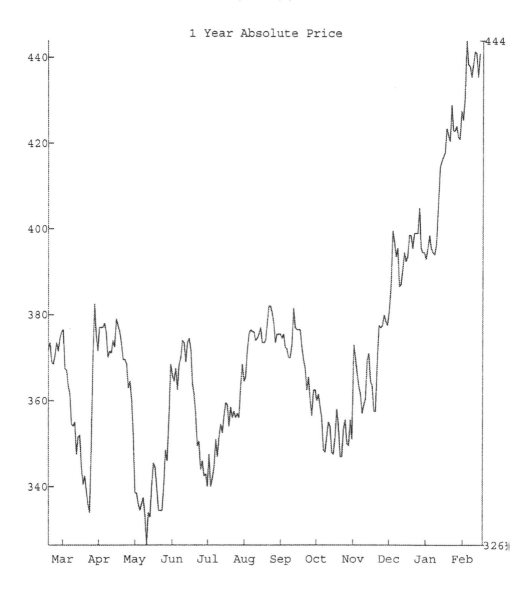

1 Year Absolute Price

that they will be considerably better (or worse) than those which the market is expecting.

Rather than sit and wait for a sudden rise or fall in the share price (which may or may not occur), all you need to do is to instruct your stockbroker to sell the shares at a certain price if they reach that level during the day, or week, or month. This is known as a 'limit order' and you can leave it in place for as long as you want. You can cancel it at any time you wish, thereby taking control for the decision to sell back into your own hands. There should be no charge for this service. It is particularly useful if you are going to be unavailable or unable to get to a telephone at the critical time when you think that the share price may move substantially, whether in your favour or against you, and it is important that you either capture the profit from the rise in price, or limit your loss if it starts to fall out of bed.

To be a successful short-term trader, do I have to know a lot about the companies whose shares I might buy?

No. A short-term trader is not interested in whether the company makes bicycles, bottle tops or battleships. All he or she is interested in is whether the share price is fluctuating *regularly and considerably* over reasonably short periods. It is the pattern which is important because if a share has been oscillating consistently in price over the recent past, it becomes a reasonable bet that it will continue so to do. Remember that your capital is exposed to risk at all times when it is sitting in a share. The risk ceases when you have sold the share and received cash back in exchange. So what you are trying to achieve is an investment for a short time in a share where you stand the greatest chance of making a small profit. When you have got the profit, you sell the share and take it, together with your capital, back into your own hand and eliminate the risk until the next time. One of the problems confronting you will always be the question of how long it will take for the share to perform to your requirements.

'A short-term trader is not interested in whether the company makes bicycles, bottle tops or battleships.'

13

■ EXAMPLE: Anglo United

Let me give you an example of an out-and-out gamble which occurred early in 1996. The story is interesting because very often you will get 'red hot tips' from all sorts of sources and you have to learn how to evaluate risk as well as time. I call the latter the 'exposure risk', which is quite different from the risk of loss through the share price falling out of bed. The longer you are open to the exposure risk, the more chance you have of loss through a drop in the share price (capital risk), so the two are linked but just occasionally you can't avoid a long exposure risk as well.

The company is called Anglo United, and in February 1996 the record of its performance was abysmal. Not only had it not paid a dividend for some years, but it had been making losses which increased year after year.

The price of the share was ¼p bid (to sell), and ¾p offered (to buy). Since the price is likely to move in ¼p amounts, the capital risk was huge. If the price dropped at all the spread would probably have moved to 0p bid, and ½p offered. In market jargon it would have been quoted as 'offered only'. In other words, you would be unable to sell the share at all because no market maker was prepared to buy the stock at any price.

Now if you had looked at the chart of the share, you would have seen no movement at all over the previous 12 months, and prior to that, the picture was enough to put anyone off – just a straight downward sloping line.

I have said that a trader is not interested in what the company makes (apart from profits!) and 99 times out of 100 any research would have stopped right there. But the advice to have a look at the company came from someone whose opinion I respect, so I looked a bit further.

Apart from the terrible record of losses and complete absence of dividends, the business in which the company was involved was dying. Originally the company had been called the Coalite Company and it still manufactures briquettes for burning in solid fuel furnaces both in the domestic heating and kitchen markets as well as for generating electricity. It had been a profitable business because coal dust was cheap to obtain. But with the restrictions imposed on burning coal for environmental reasons, and the growth of oil and gas-fired and electrically operated domestic appliances, the market was in terminal decline.

In addition to this horrendous story, there was one other item which begged an enormous question. The company had debts to its bankers of about £390 million. Now why would the hard-nosed banks be prepared to live with such huge liabilities for so long where their debtor was involved in a dying industry without being able to make a profit for several years and with no apparent likelihood of ever being able to recover?

The answer lay in the list of the company's assets. It owned the Falkland Islands Company which in turn owned a large chunk of the Falkland Islands, including Port Stanley. Now this asset was not very exciting because nothing much happens in the Falkland Islands, apart from the recent warfare with its usual destruction of buildings and disruption of such trade as there might be and the consequent expensive and costly reconstruction. But upon further enquiry, I discovered that the sea bed around the Falkland Islands bears a remarkable similarity to that in the North Sea. So the perceived solution had to be that the banks were supporting the company in the hope that there would be large quantities of oil to be extracted from the surrounding sea bed and that Port Stanley might become another Aberdeen.

Now how do you evaluate the risk both as to capital and exposure? Even if the banks did not pull the rug from under Anglo United, it only needed an adverse report from the oil exploration companies, or a further military threat from Argentina, for the whole company to go belly up. So how much money should anyone invest in such a gamble?

There is absolutely no doubt that any money used to buy shares in such a situation should be regarded as lost from the moment the decision to purchase was made. There should be no difference between investing in such an out and out gamble such as this one or putting the same amount of money into the Lottery. There would be no chance of cutting your losses. It is certainly not the sort of investment anyone should make who cannot afford to lose the whole lot without feeling the pinch. If you have to ask yourself if you can afford it, then you should leave it alone.

The share price did not move one iota from February 1996 until March 1997 (over 12 months), when it suddenly jumped to 2¼p bid and 2¾p offered. I shall leave it to you to work out what percentage increase that is. It was well worth having. The next question is, should you hold on to the shares if you had bought them at 3/4p, or, if you had only just heard about them, should you buy them at the current price?

The story in the example illustrates the conflict between fear and greed rather well. On the one hand, if you are sitting on a considerable profit, but are attracted to the thought that there might be more to come, you might say that any slippage in the share price will give you the chance to get out with less of a profit, but still some profit. Against that, I would argue, the price is just as likely to fall back to its previous levels in one move if it rose in such a manner. On the other hand, if you are a newcomer to the stock, can you expect to see the rise being sustained in the same proportion as the last increase? I do not think that the risk factors have been reduced in any way, and if anyone wanted to buy in at the current price, all the comments made above about the share being an absolute gamble remain undiluted.

There is an old adage in the City:

'It never pays to try to have two bites at the cherry'.

All the information which I have described above can be found from reading the Extel card, and this applies to any company listed on the London Stock Exchange. You should be able to get one for any company in which you become interested by asking your stockbroker to send it to you.

Generally, however, the trader's approach to investing is completely different to that which you need to adopt as a long-term Investor.

There is nothing to stop you running two portfolios concurrently, i.e. short-term trading and long-term investing, and in fact most people do buy shares for the two separate objectives, but most people confuse the disciplines required to be successful in either one or the other with the result that they do not make the sort of profits which they could do.

It is of paramount importance, and can not be stressed too strongly, that you separate your approach to both. It is for this reason that I recommend that you keep your short-term trading portfolio quite separate from your long-term investment portfolio, and that you run them both as two completely independent businesses. They should each have their own performance targets and be reviewed at regular intervals to see whether they are meeting or surpassing or falling short of the goals which you have set for them. This is the professional approach which is the only way to run your own investments successfully. The amateur carries out sporadic reviews and then wonders why he or she has missed the bus and is left feeling sorry and hurt.

The best simile which I can think of is to regard your capital invested as if it is a business. Suppose you were to buy a pub or a petrol station instead of shares. You would expect the business to provide you with an income as well as increase in value, so that if you had to sell it you would get back more than you paid when you bought it. The point is that you would consider it quite normal to set daily or weekly or monthly targets for the income which it must

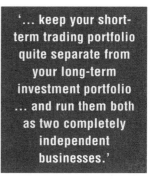

'... keep your short-term trading portfolio quite separate from your long-term investment portfolio ... and run them both as two completely independent businesses.'

produce for you to be able to pay your bills and to live. There is absolutely no difference in that respect between investing in a commercial business and investing in shares. It always amazes me that so few people plan their stockmarket investments in a planned and structured way. It is as if they feel that they have no control over the fluctuations in the values of their portfolios and that their invested wealth is rather like flotsam: ebbing and flowing with the tide. You *can* manage your capital efficiently and if you don't, you have no one else to blame but yourself. All it takes is a little bit of time and some application.

These reviews do not have to take up a lot of your time. It is not so much the amount of time that is spent as the fact that you set aside sufficient time to carry out your review regularly. The best way to organise your daily schedule is to download all the share prices into your PC every day at the same time, as well as reading the financial Press as early in the day as possible.

Recent surveys have shown that the average investor spends two hours a week considering his or her portfolio. I have to say that I find it extraordinary that only two hours are spent reviewing something so vital and important as the performance of one's liquid assets, but if that is all the time which is available, then it becomes even more essential that such limited time is put to the best possible use. With IT so cheap and widely available, there is no excuse for slack management of your wealth.

SUMMARY

In this chapter we have described:

- What is meant by short-term trading

- How short short-term is

- What the objectives of short-term trading are

- The ease of achieving short-term trading objectives

- The time required to monitor the performance of each investment

- How much knowledge is required of the individual companies whose shares may or may not be bought.

MENTAL ATTITUDE AND DISCIPLINES REQUIRED

INTRODUCTION

I have devoted a full chapter to explaining what sort of mental attitude is required in the approach to short-term trading because it is so important. The disciplines which are needed stem from the mental attitude and a lot of people find it difficult to begin with to stick to them. However, you will ignore them at your peril and the truly professional investor will make more money (and lose less) than those who let their heart rule their head.

In this chapter we explain:

- the importance of following the 'numbers'
- the importance of buying or selling when the chart dictates action
- the necessity to control 'the greed factor'.

It is a moot point whether the ability to make money is an art or craft, and whether it can be taught, or whether one is born with it. Both views have their adherents and much time and energy has been expended in arguing the opposing opinions.

However, what is quite clear is that whether you find the process easy to achieve or hard work, the most important element for a trader is to eliminate all emotional involvement from your decision-making. You need to have an approach which is ruthless and calculating. Bury any feelings of like or dislike towards the company or its business. Whether it is involved in manufacturing or distributing products or services which you find pleasant or abhorrent is totally immaterial. You are out to make money and nothing else.

Thus your mental attitudes must be governed by cold mathematics and demonstrable measurements only. You must be prepared to stick to decisions as to when to buy and to sell which are based entirely on the actual movements of share prices measured both in money and percentage terms, and nothing else.

We shall come to the greed factor later, but so often I see people hanging on to a share when it has passed its peak price and refusing to sell until (they hope) it gets back to somewhere near its previous high with the inevitable result that they lose more than they need have done. Likewise, many times do I recommend a share to clients who say that they will watch the price, and if it continues to rise they will buy the share. What on earth is the point of that? Either the share is worth buying for a particular reason, or it is not. If the system says 'buy', then the sooner you are in the share the better. Someone once said that 'Patience may be a virtue, but impatience can frequently be profitable'.

> '... your mental attitudes must be governed by cold mathematics and demonstrable measurements only.'

So before we get to describing how you read the signals, and how you set your targets for performance, let us understand and spell out the principles by which you will operate your short-term trading disciplines.

TRENDS

You will select *only* shares which have an established and demonstrable upward trend.

What is a trend?

We have established the fact that share prices almost never remain static. Although they will fluctuate regularly, it is important to establish whether the overall direction is going up, down, or in essence going nowhere.

There are many reasons for such fluctuations. Excessive demand, with a corresponding lack of supply will push the price up. Lower than expected profits will lead to share dumping and the price will drop, and so on. Frequently, however, the overall direction will follow the market as a whole.

Thus you need to see in which direction the share prices are going. You will see why it is necessary to measure the past performance over two years at least so that you can get a more accurate history to help you in your decision-making.

Does a trend matter?

This may seem a facile question but there are two reasons why I have posed it.

The first is to remind you that the ability to see an overall picture of the history of a share is a very useful aid in your decision-making. It should not be the sole factor, but you disregard it at your peril.

The second is to emphasise the need to remember the basic truths about what makes share prices alter. They are:

a) Market opinion

The market opinion dictates the popularity or otherwise of a share. Such opinion is generated by Press and analytical comment, particularly with regard to the future earnings of the company. Good or bad Press comment will generate interest in the share, and the more frequently such comment is published, the more the share price is in the limelight. Sometimes the market opinion of one share will be influenced by what is happening to another share, or the whole sector may be rising or falling in popularity. For example, if it is perceived that there may be a glut of oil building up (because of a very mild winter perhaps), then the market opinion of oil shares in general will be bearish and all the oil shares are likely to be marked down – the good ones as well as the bad.

b) Investor demand

Investor demand will generally be fuelled by Press comment. Investors will want to buy a popular share because financial journalists are strongly recommending it. So the more people buy a share because it has been tipped, the more they will chase the share price upwards. Likewise, they will want to dump a share which is receiving bad Press comment and this will depress the share price. It is very difficult to quantify investor demand. Even when one has access to the sophisticated data services in the City, you can not be sure that the reports of each trade which are exhibited on the dealing screens refer to a large institutional sale or purchase, or whether they are the result of market makers adjusting their books by trading between themselves. Nevertheless it is possible to get a 'feel' about an unusual movement in a share price and you should ask your broker to find out what the market thinks about a particular share before you buy it.

> **TIP** **It is worth remembering that the very nature of the stock market is to behave in an 'excessive' way**. It generally over reacts to both good and bad news. The pendulum swings too far in either direction, and when the market has gone down far enough so that the quality shares look cheap, very often that is the time to buy. The same thing is true in reverse. When the market has reached new heights, you should think about selling. Within reason, you should aim to buy when everyone else is selling, and sell when everyone else is buying. But you need to do so *within the established trading range of each individual share*. Think of the market as a whole, and each individual share in particular, as if it were the tide. You want to buy at the end of the ebb when it has just turned, and you want to sell at the top of the flood, if possible, just after it has turned.

Since memory is notoriously fallible, it helps if there is some way of prompting you to investigate the reasons for any abnormal or dramatic change in the historical pattern of progression of a share price. A chart will enable you to see when such changes occurred and so you can concentrate your research on the information which was published around the appropriate dates. It may be that substantial changes occurred for reasons which had nothing to do with the perceived earnings potential of the company, such as the crash of 1987 or the outbreak of war in the Middle East, but at least you will have satisfied yourself as to whether the reason was pertinent to the market as a whole or that share in particular. If, for example, the share which you are investigating dropped in price substantially on an occasion and your subsequent research showed that the rest of the market remained unaltered, you would definitely want to find out the reason why the fall occurred.

Thus the overall trend, if measured over a sufficiently long period, will show you what the general market consensus is. In the case of a demonstrable falling trend, you need to have very good reasons for believing that the market has got it wrong for one particular share over such a long time, if *you* think that the trend is going to be reversed and sustained.

It goes without saying that you will only be interested in considering a share whose price is on an upward trend. It is just conceivable that you might look at a share with a downward trend, but only if you had extremely good reasons for doing so, such as concrete knowledge that some news was about to be released which would reverse the current direction. If that were the case, and the knowledge was so secret that no-one in the market was aware of it, you would be in possession of what is called 'insider information'. If you were to buy the share you would be guilty of insider dealing, and liable to the possibility of a custodial sentence and the certainty of a fine. The same penalties would apply if the trend was rising.

> '... as a rule of thumb, the higher the rate of trend, the better for the trader.'

However, it makes much more sense to choose only those shares whose trend is positive, because the chances are that in the short-term the trend will continue in the same direction. Since we are only concerned with the short-term situation, those are the shares which we want to isolate.

Does the rate of trend matter?

A share whose historic price record is showing a strong and sustained upward trend is more likely to enable you to reach your target profit level sooner than one which is showing a more gentle rising slope. Later on in the book, we shall demonstrate the effect of this fact when we come to setting achievable targets and how to calculate them, but for the present suffice it to say that as a rule of thumb, the higher the rate of trend, the better for the trader.

How do I find which shares have an upward trend?

You will see two illustrations of trends in Figure 2.1 and Figure 2.2.

Figure 2.1 is the chart of the share price of Boots on a closing daily mid-price basis for the five-year period December 1992 to early November 1996.

Fig 2.1 Boots: share price on a closing daily mid-price basis December 1992 to early November 1996

(Source: Topic)

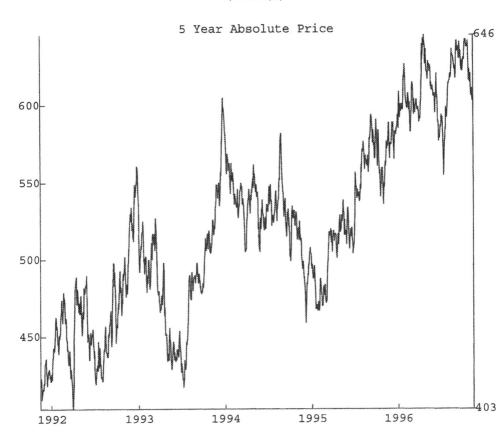

5 Year Absolute Price

There are several lessons to be learned from this chart, and they are as follows.

From about February 1995 until about March 1996 the trend line was rising at a fast rate. Since then, it has continued to rise, albeit more slowly, and so the share would qualify for consideration for a trader.

The other lessons to be learned concern the measurement of the trading range, the effects of a 'double bottom', and a 'head and shoulders' appearing in a chart. The latter two aspects will be explained in detail further on in this part.

Fig 2.2 Boots: share price on a daily basis mid-December 1995 to mid-November 1996

(Source: Topic)

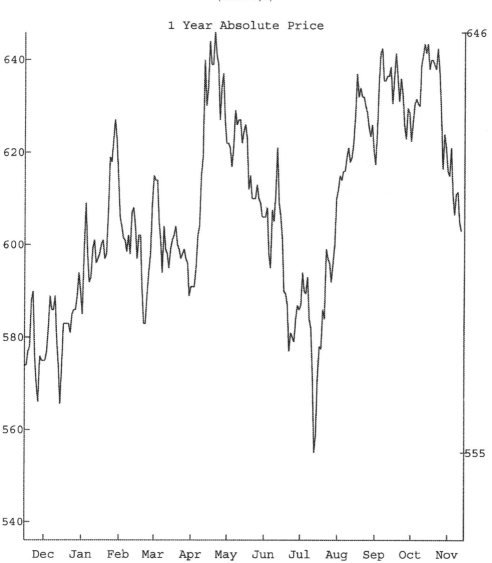

1 Year Absolute Price

27

Figure 2.2 shows the chart of the same share plotted on a daily basis over the period of 12 months ending mid-November 1996. From a short term trading point of view, this chart is more informative and it is easier to make more accurate predictions concerning the likely behaviour of the share price and to quantify the probable increase in share value.

Let us see what Figure 2.2 has to tell us.

The trend line is very important as we have shown, but we have to be sure that the picture is not misleading. If the period over which the trend line is being measured is too short, it may be that what appears to be a rising trend is, in fact, only a 'blip' in an otherwise falling trend when measured over a longer time span. You really need to measure the trend line over a minimum of six months to be sure of the established direction which the trend line is taking.

Figure 2.3 for another company shows you how dangerous it can be to base your conclusions on looking at too short a period. If you were only to look at the picture shown within the box, you would assume that the behaviour of the share price (which establishes the trend) was set to continue its rise to reach the previous 'high' and perhaps rise a bit further. However, when you look at the overall picture recorded over a longer period, you will realise that the actual trend is downwards, so you should expect the next 'high' to be below that of the last one, if the longer-term trend is to be maintained.

How do I use a trend for my target setting?

Figure 2.4 shows the trend of General Accident over the last three years. Let us take each year in rotation and assume that we are starting this exercise at the *end* of Year 1. The starting point is July 1996, and we have decided that this share looks like one which will show us a good profit if the established trend continues.

Starting from July 1994, the share price line cut the vertical axis at 490p. At the end of the year, the line cut the vertical axis at 605p. Thus the *trend* line showed an annual rise of 115p which is equivalent to 23.46 per cent.

So at the beginning of Year 2, we are assuming that the rate of rise will continue unchanged.

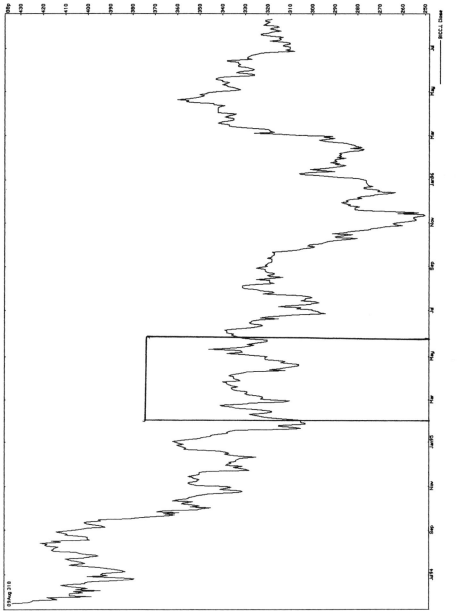

Fig 2.3 Concealed downward trend
(Source: Reuters)

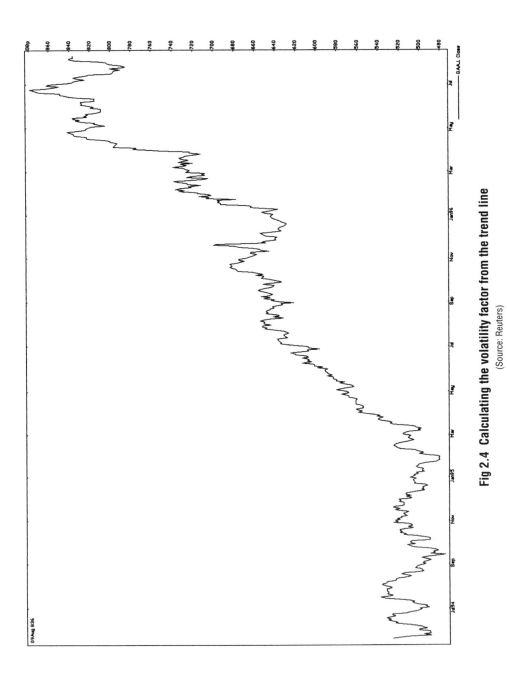

Fig 2.4 Calculating the volatility factor from the trend line

(Source: Reuters)

That is to say that if we are considering a purchase of this share at 605p, we are expecting to see the value rise to 746p within 12 months.

$$605p + \frac{24}{100} \times 605p) = 746p$$

In fact, the share price rose to about 838p in July 1996, although it had been higher (about 878p) in June that year. Nevertheless, the increase over the previous 12 months amounted to 273p or 45.12 per cent.

Thus you can see that the rate of rise in the trend has accelerated from 23.46 per cent to 45.12 per cent.

Now whilst this share price has been steadily rising from one year's end to the next, the actual daily movement will be fluctuating up and down. If you take the *average* of these short-term rises and falls when you carry out a similar analytical exercise for other companies to which you are attracted, you can establish the degree of volatility of each share over very short periods.

The movement of the share price above and below the average line is called the 'volatility factor' and this must not be confused with the trend. You must deal with each item separately, and we explain volatility and the part it has to play later on in the book. So the first calculation to be established is this.

On the record of the share to date (over the last 12 months), it is reasonable to expect that an investment in this share will appreciate by x per cent.

You set your target for growth for the next 12 months by multiplying the current price by the percentage increase achieved over the last 12 months and adding the resulting figure to the current price.

> Your anticipated growth calculations are based on fact, not hope, and they should be achievable because you have used historic data rather than wild assumptions.

31

What can go wrong with this assumption?

Obviously there are many factors which will affect the market attitude to a share, such as an unexpected drop in earnings, a change in management, a perceived danger or threat to its markets, a rise in interest rates etc., but generally for the short-term trader these worries are of less importance than they are for the long-term investor because the trader is not expecting to be exposed to these risks for very long.

Nevertheless, any such potential threats should be borne in mind at all times and the likelihood of any of them occurring to inflict damage should be evaluated *before* you commit yourself.

So the first lesson of short-term trading is to moderate your desires for profit to a degree which is reasonable and achievable.

The second lesson is that by following this discipline you are creating actual price forecasts with which to establish a budget or control index for monitoring the performance of the trend of that particular share over the next few months. This way, you have removed a large amount of the guesswork from forecasting.

Obviously, the trend line for each share will have different historic rates of increase and so you must go through the calculations for each one to see whether the rate of rise is satisfactory to your requirements in terms of achievable profit.

> '... the first lesson of short-term trading is to moderate your desires for profit to a degree which is reasonable and achievable.'

The way in which this is achieved is to use moving averages and to establish trading ranges.

The establishment of trend lines, and the consequent ability to calculate levels of both support and resistance in the future for a share price is so important that it is examined in greater detail in Chapter 5 under the heading *Technical analysis*.

MOVING AVERAGES

A moving average is created as follows:

Add together the share prices for a number of days (say, 30) and

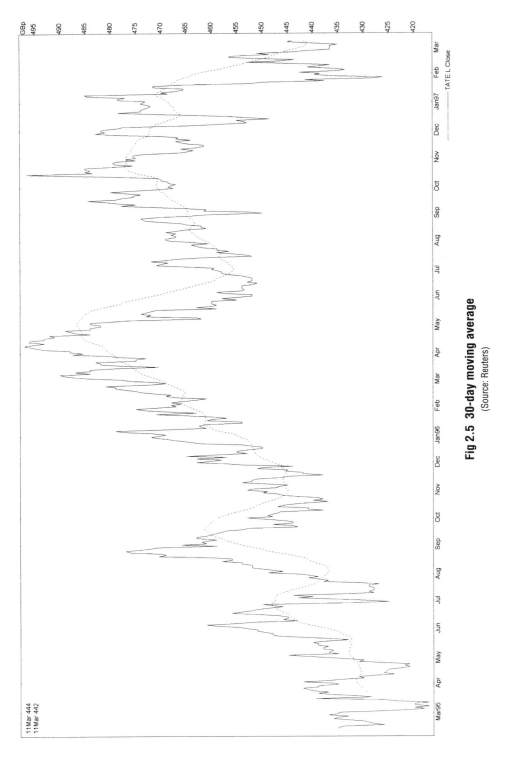

Fig 2.5 30-day moving average
(Source: Reuters)

33

divide the sum by the number of days. Plot the resulting figure on the graph, or chart, on the 30th day. On the 31st day, add the share price for that day to the previous total (making a sum of 31 days' prices), and subtract the first day's price (bringing the sum back to 30 days' total) and divide the new sum by 30 to give you the new 30-day average. Plot the new average price on the chart on the 31st day. Continue to do this every day so that you build up a new line on the chart which, in this case, would be called the 30-day moving average line.

Figure 2.5 shows the chart of Tate & Lyle over the period March 1995 to March 1997 with the 30-day moving average superimposed.

Before you give up at this point and say that this all seems like too much time-consuming hard work, do not worry. There are several ways of getting this done without spending time or energy doing it yourself. However, it is one of the most important tools which you will need to employ to be successful in making the profits which you want, so it is important that you understand how a moving average is constructed.

You can use any number of days to produce a moving average, but the usual ones employed by the professionals are 30 days and 90 days. The method of construction is the same whatever period you choose to use.

Figure 2.6 shows the chart of Tate & Lyle over the same period, with the 90-day moving average superimposed.

Figure 2.7 shows the chart for Tate & Lyle with both the 30-day and 90-day averages superimposed.

How are they used?

Although a moving average has some of the same characteristics as a trend line, you should not confuse the two. A 30-day moving average will show you the general direction in which the share price is moving over a short period, whilst the 90-day one will do the same over a longer period. The trend line gives you the overall direction of the share price from one year to the next. You will have noted that the share price can follow an arc during the year, ending up at a higher

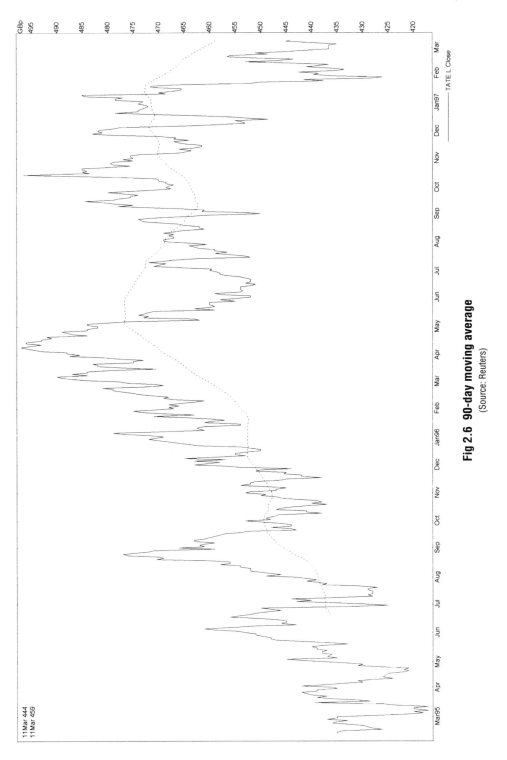

Fig 2.6 90-day moving average
(Source: Reuters)

35

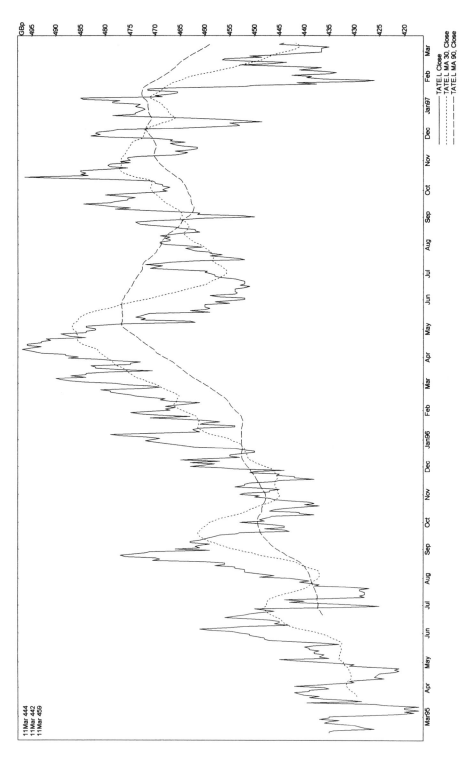

Fig 2.7 30-day and 90-day moving average

(Source: Reuters)

level than that at which it started. If such a picture emerges, you would be perfectly correct in saying that the trend is upward. However, during the year, the price will almost certainly rise and fall whilst following the overall trend, and it is for these reasons that you need to superimpose average price movements over shorter periods.

What can they tell you?

If the 30-day moving average line cuts through the 90-day line in a downward direction **and they are both moving in a downward direction,** then you can expect the share price to fall and probably by a long way. If the 30-day line cuts downwards through the 90-day line while the 90-day line is moving horizontally, or better still in an upward direction, the reduction in the share price will probably be fairly small.

If the 30-day moving average line cuts upwards through the 90-day line **while it is also rising,** the share price will rise considerably.

Never forget that these indicators are only tools which should be used to check whether what seems like a good investment is in fact being masked by adverse trends or potential changes in direction which could cost you dear. You should always use them in your 'sifting' process to identify whether this is the right moment to buy a share, or to sell one which you hold. They are some of the checks and balances which should be part of your armoury, and it ought to become an automatic process which you go through without thinking about it.

VOLATILITY

It is very rare for the price of a share to move upwards or downwards in a straight line. Normally it will move in a series of short rises and falls. Some share prices remain static for days or even weeks on end without moving at all. However the general pattern looks more like a zigzag progression.

Consequently, this volatility in the share price means that during a period a record emerges of the 'high' and the 'low' value which the share achieves. In some cases the *degree* of volatility is considerable, and in others it is insignificant. The short-term trader should be looking for a share where the degree of volatility is as large as possible, over the shortest possible time *and* which is being repeated at regular intervals.

Refer back to Figure 2.2 for an example of a really superb opportunity for trading. This share pattern is a trader's delight. A purchase in early January 1996 at around 565p would have been held until February and sold after it had turned downwards. Assume the holding was sold at 620p (after it had turned down from its 'high' of about 628p), and the gross profit would have been 55p or 9.73 per cent. Then if the share had been repurchased at the beginning of March after it had turned upwards at, say, 587p (from the previous 'low' of about 584p), you would have held it until it had turned down from the 'high' in May of 646p. Assume that you sold it at 640p, you would have made a gross profit of 53p, or 10.05 per cent. If you had waited to repurchase the share until the end of July or early August after it had turned upwards from its 'low' of 555p, and say that you bought in at 560p, you would have held it until the end of October or early November and sold after it had turned down from its 'high' of about 642p. Assume that you had sold at 638p, you would have made a profit of 78p or 13.92 per cent before costs.

Thus within the space of nine months you could have made a gross profit of 186p per share at an average purchase price of 570.66p, which is equivalent to 32.59 per cent. Even when you take into consideration dealing costs for both buying and selling and government stamp duty on each purchase, the resulting net profit is well worth having.

If you had held the share for the full 12 months in your portfolio, having bought it at around 575p at the beginning of the period, the holding would have appreciated to about 602p at the end of the 12 months which we are looking at, or a rise of 27p which is equivalent to 4.69 per cent.

However, there is one very important lesson for a trader to be learned here. When the share price starts to fall, get out. There is an old saying in the stockmarket: 'The first cut is the cheapest cut'. It is a common failing among most non-professional investors to hang on to a share whose price has fallen to a level below that which they paid for it in the hope that the share price will recover sufficiently to let them get out without loss.

Figure 2.8 shows the chart of Tate & Lyle which illustrates these criteria very well also and shows that it is not just the smaller companies which are candidates for trading in.

The short-term trader is particularly interested in being able to measure the volatility over very short periods because this information will indicate whether there is sufficient room within the oscillation to make the percentage increase which is needed in order to cover both the target profit as well as the dealing costs. Thus some system of measurement is needed which allows the short-term trader to see quickly whether a particular share has the potential to deliver the goods or not.

> '... there is one very important lesson for a trader to be learned here. When the share price starts to fall, get out.'

The way in which this is achieved is to use moving averages and to establish trading ranges.

TRADING RANGES

Historic

Trading ranges, combined with volatility of share price movement are the two most important factors to establish for the trader. A share price which is moving up and down like a yo-yo is exactly what is wanted to create good profit opportunities, and the second ingredient to give you the greatest chance of success is the measurement of the trading range.

The way to establish what is the trading range is to draw two parallel lines (they *must* be parallel) between the 'peaks' and the 'troughs' of the price shown on the chart.

Fig 2.8 Tate & Lyle: share price March 1996 to February 1997
(Source: Topic)

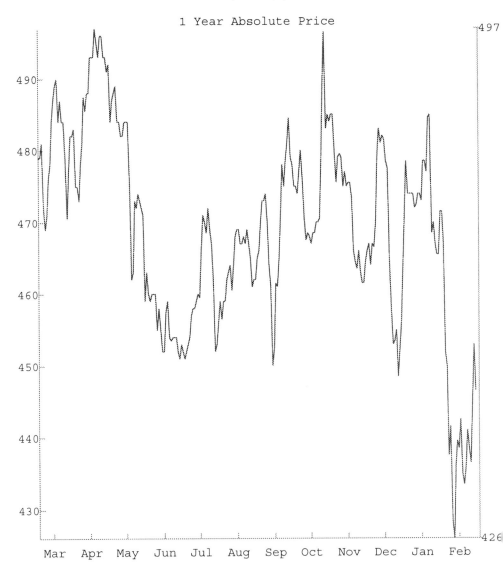

Figure 2.9 is the five-year chart of BT from February 1992 to February 1997 with the trading ranges drawn in.

You can see that they bear little resemblance to the trend line (not shown) over the period, but they do let you see the degree of volatility in the share price. In addition, they give you one other most important benefit. They enable you to calculate the rise and fall above and below the trend at the time during the various periods shown. They also show you when is the best time to buy and to sell. Thus, by combining the rate of trend and superimposing the trading range, you can set a realistic and achievable profit target for your capital to achieve.

However, it is all very well to look backwards over a five year period. The trader will be looking forward over a much shorter timescale.

Figure 2.10 shows the historic performance over the last 12 months ending mid-February 1997, with the trading ranges added. The picture that emerges is interesting because what was a fairly flat trend from March to December, suddenly changed direction dramatically and became one which was rising rapidly for the last three months.

Forecasting the future

When a share price breaks upwards through the trading range and does not fall back to its previous levels, you are in unknown territory. It is perfectly natural for a share price to pause for a while after a big rise but the trader should wait to see what sort of a new pattern emerges before making a decision. If you hold the share in your portfolio, keep it until the price drops and then sell it. Watch the price of such a share like a hawk, because it *can* drop just as fast as it has risen. You don't want to miss out on the rise in price, but equally you don't want to see the gain disappear before your eyes.

Also, the degree of volatility can often reduce when compared with recent past performance. The effect is to make it look as if the share has lost its sense of direction and its momentum. This situation is probably one of the most common that you will encounter when trawling through the charts of all the companies listed on the market.

PART 1 · TRADING

Fig 2.9 BT: February 1992 to February 1997 with trading ranges
(Source: Topic)

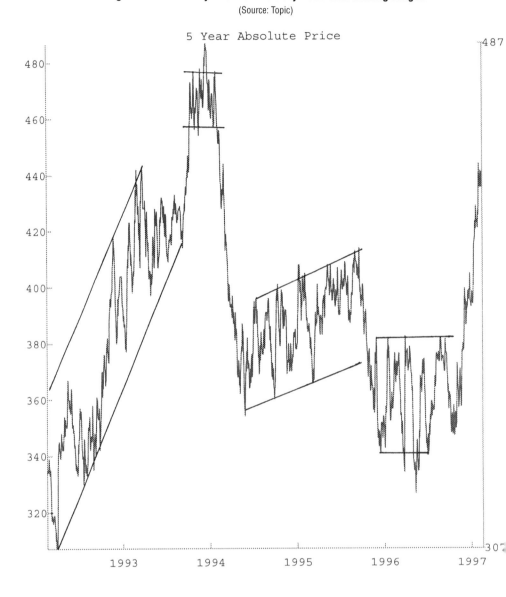

42

Fig 2.10 BT: March 1996 to February 1997 with trading ranges
(Source: Topic)

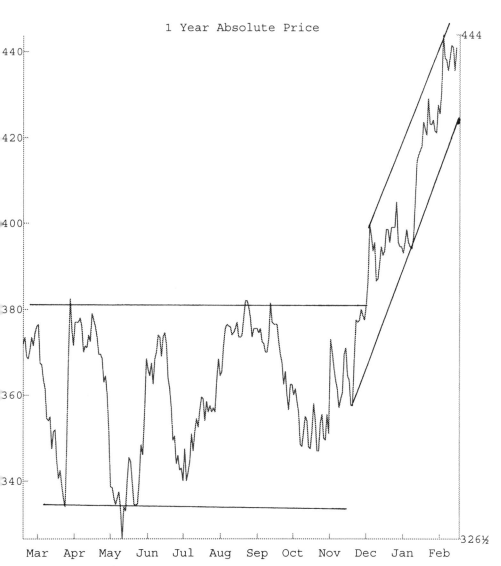

43

Fig 2.11 Example of funnel effect
(Source: Topic)

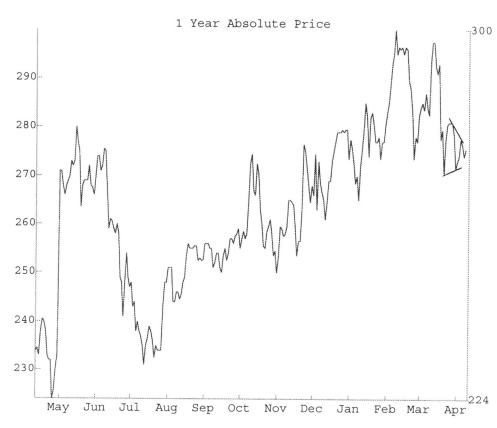

Figure 2.11 illustrates this point very well. It is most obvious when the recent 'highs' are getting lower, and the recent 'lows' are getting higher. If you draw a line through the 'highs' and 'lows' you get a funnel effect with the two lines appearing to converge at some stage in the near future.

What does this mean?

Generally this means that the investor interest in this share is disappearing. It does not mean that the market sentiment has changed, but because the volume of trade in that particular share is dropping, the share price has become less volatile. If there had been a preponderance of buyers or sellers, and if that volume of activity had been mostly one way, the direction of the share price would reflect it: more persistent sellers than buyers, then the price would drop; more persistent buyers than sellers, then the price would rise. However, it is not in the nature of share prices to remain static (unless there is no demand at all for the share), and so you must wait and see in which direction the price begins to establish a new trend. When such a configuration occurs, the risk element increases substantially, because you have no way of forecasting which way the price is going to go, nor have you got any trend line to use as a basis for prediction. I strongly recommend that you do not buy a share which is exhibiting such characteristics. If you hold the share in your portfolio anyway, then you should be prepared to get out quickly if the share price drops below the last 'low'.

TIP **When you see such a picture emerging from the chart of the market as a whole *after* a sustained bull run, it usually means that the next move is going to be downwards.** It may well be worth a gamble at that point to buy a put option on the futures market to hedge against any losses which you might incur in shares held within your portfolio which have not yet risen in value sufficiently to give you your target profits. Likewise, after a sustained fall in the market as a whole, when you see a similar picture on the chart you might buy a call option to participate in the future recovery. Remember what I have said about the market over-reacting and behaving like a pendulum?

It is just as important to protect your capital by getting out early and taking a small loss as it is to make profits. If you look after the losses, the profits will look after themselves.

'Double bottoms' and 'head and shoulders'

These are descriptions given to certain configurations which sometimes occur on graphs or charts of historic share prices. They can often signal a change in direction which may well be dramatic and experience in translating the messages will prove beneficial.

Double bottom

When a share price has reached a 'low', recovered to a price above the low point and then dropped back to the same 'low' again, *if it then turns upwards* the price will almost invariably climb upwards and continue to do so.

Figure 2.12 shows such an event and it is by no means an uncommon occurrence. You will realise that a double bottom represents a 'buy' signal but you should not act on it until the share price has turned upwards in case the graph does not configure a double bottom but merely reports a hiccup in what turns out to be a steady downward trend.

> 'A double bottom can alert you to the strong likelihood of a sustained recovery in the share price.'

Fig 2.12 Double bottom
(Source: Topic)

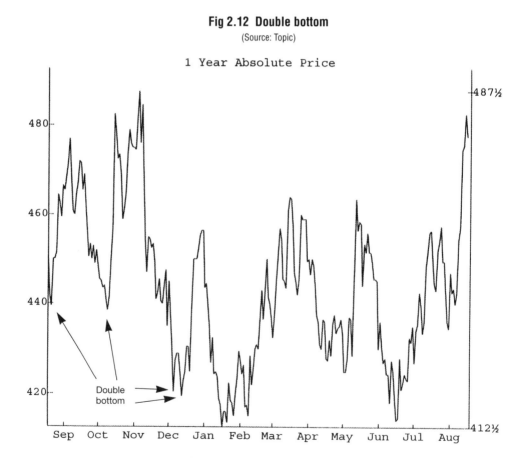

1 Year Absolute Price

There are many reasons for the price behaving in such a manner and when the chart indicates that a double bottom has occurred it is well worth speaking to your broker to find out whether there are any rumours which might indicate that the company is under a cloud, in the opinion of the market, before you commit yourself.

If there are no apparent reasons for the second drop in the price, wait until it has turned upwards and then buy the share. The double bottoms may not be close to each other in time. They could be several weeks apart. It is the configuration which matters and which should alert you to the strong likelihood of a sustained recovery in the share price.

Head and shoulders

Whereas a double bottom is usually the precursor of a rise in a share price, a head and shoulders indicates the opposite. Figure 2.13 demonstrates what a head and shoulders looks like on a chart and you will see that the shape is unmistakable. A head and shoulders does not always result in a sustained fall, but the price may take longer to recover than you had planned for your short-term trading performance target.

It may occur at a time between your purchase of the share and while the price is rising to hit the pre-set target which you have chosen. If so, then you would probably be better advised to dump the share and find another to buy because the chances are that you may have to wait for a considerable time for the share price to turn upwards again and resume its climb. Also there is a strong possibility that the share price may continue to drop and wipe out any gain which you may have achieved already. Remember that the first cut is the cheapest cut!

Fig 2.13 Head and shoulders

(Source: Topic)

1 Year Absolute Price

SUMMARY

In this chapter we have looked at the mental attitude you require to be a short-term trader, and the disciplines you should follow.

- We have explained that for trading purposes, you must not get emotionally involved in the individual shares which you buy and sell.
- We have demonstrated the need to set short-term targets which are achievable and realistic based on data arising out of historic performance for each individual share.
- We have shown that your decisions to buy and sell are dictated solely by the share price movement within certain measurements and that you stick rigidly to the chart information and abide by the criteria which the chart dictates.
- We have described how to use the moving averages so that they act as a reinforcement of your investment decision, or so that they alert you to possible dangers before making the investment and consequently save you from loss.
- We have stressed the importance of establishing trading ranges for the historical share price performance and the use of this tool in setting targets both as to the amount of profit to be expected and the time it should take to materialise.
- We have shown how important are the trading range tool combined with the need to find shares with maximum volatility in the share price over short periods to achieve the greatest profits.
- We have demonstrated the need to keep greed under control.

CONTROL SYSTEMS FOR DATA ANALYSIS AND PORTFOLIO MANAGEMENT

INTRODUCTION

All my research shows that the private investor operating from home wants the following facilities:

- hassle-free share price updating methods which are quick and easy to operate
- a simple data processing system
- inexpensive and reliable equipment and software.

In this chapter we describe what equipment you need to trade successfully. There is no point in spending hours and hours recording numbers by hand, analysing the data and selecting shares to buy, particularly when you may well be expecting to hold them for a relatively short period anyway.

If you were to attempt to do all that is required manually, you would need the product of several rain forests by way of paper and there would probably be no time for sleep either. You would spend so much time working things out that you would miss the opportunities anyway.

HARDWARE

So the answer is to equip yourself with a computer. Computer prices are falling weekly and the equipment which would have been uneconomic for most ordinary investors is now readily available at prices which are easily affordable.

The minimum specifications which you need for one which will work quickly are as follows:

- 8Mb RAM
- 60K hard disk space available
- VGA screen with colour
- IBM compatible
- an inkjet or laser printer.
- a telephone modem attached.

Nowadays you should be able to buy a set-up combining all these minimum requirements for under £1,000. The faster the computer and telephone modem, the fewer costs you will incur in obtaining share price data daily.

When you choose a computer, it is important to find one which will accept the software which you will require for recording share prices and analysis work. The choice will be individual, but it would probably be better to avoid Amstrad and Apple Macintosh because they are not generally compatible with IBM or *Windows*. It is generally accepted that it is better to buy new equipment rather than second-hand, if for no other reason than the ready availability of a helpline. You may have difficulty in obtaining assistance if your name was not registered at the time of the original purchase.

There are over 3,300 shares listed on the London Stock Exchange and there are about 4,500 unit trusts in addition. Since unit trusts are not traded on the stockmarket, their prices are not recorded from the same source in the database as are the share prices. It is anticipated that this situation will change when most of the UK-based unit trusts will become known as open-ended investment companies (OEICs) and prices will be made by the market makers rather than only by the individual fund managers, as is the case at present. When that change has taken place, the unit trust prices will become available from the same source as share prices are at present.

'The faster the computer and telephone modem, the fewer costs you will incur in obtaining share price data daily.'

SOFTWARE

You will need to have two items of data to operate your trading activities successfully.

First, you will require a database of at least two years' share prices daily for each of the 3,300 plus companies whose shares are listed on the market. The reason for this record is to enable you to see what the trend has been for each one in which you may become interested.

There are software programs available which do not come to you equipped with this information, and which leave you to compile your own historical database. They may be cheap to buy initially, but they defeat your main objective which is to have access to enough historic data over a long enough period to enable you to avoid getting an erroneous picture.

I have heard it said by some investors that they really think that they can cope with recording share price data only for those shares that they hold in their portfolio and they do not see any advantage in paying more for additional information which may be of no interest to them at present. Well, consider this situation.

If you have been following prudent portfolio management practices, you will have set targets for growth for each of your investments. Some of them may take longer to reach than others, but nevertheless you should have some idea of the performance you expect from each one.

Research has shown that the average investor on the stock exchange has a portfolio of 10 shares. So when one or more of your selections has reached its target, you should have an idea of what share to buy to continue your progress towards increasing your wealth. So let us assume that there are another 10 shares which you like and whose share price history you wish to monitor. You will be logging the share prices of 20 shares each day into your PC. So far so good and that will not take up much time.

However, suppose that you have sold one or more of your holdings and someone says to you that you really should buy the ABC company, or you read about it in a reputable journal such as the *Investors Chronicle* or the *Financial Times*, or you see a strong recommendation to get into a share in the *Penny Share Guide* or *Stock Market Confidential* or a similar tip sheet. The chances are that you will not have been recording the price movements of this company at all and so you are in the dark about its recent history or longer-term trend. You are

> 'Research has shown that the average investor on the stock exchange has a portfolio of 10 shares.'

at a distinct disadvantage compared with someone who can refer to all such data at the press of a button, so to say.

In fact, if you are armed with such information as part of the package in your software, you do not need to wait to receive any of the publications. You can browse through the share price histories at your leisure and find your own 'steamers', to use racing jargon.

One such program which I use is called *Cybertrader* and on my PC it takes about 23 seconds a day to down-load over 3,300 share prices. The cost of this daily data input is the cost of a telephone call for 23 seconds. Hardly expensive. The program does all the analysis for me automatically including revaluing each individual investment as well as the whole portfolio and updates the charts of all the shares on the London Stock Exchange. It tells me at a glance whether each share in my portfolios has risen or dropped in price since the last update and calculates automatically for me the percentage gain or loss for each holding since the date of purchase. In addition, it will alert me to any shares which have dropped to their pre-set stop loss limits. If I have told the computer to advise me when a share price has risen by the pre-set percentage gain which I have decided to be both realistic and achievable, it will only do so *after* the share price has turned down. Thus, on many occasions, I find that whereas I had been seeking a gain of say 8 per cent, the share price has continued to rise and the computer tells me to sell the share only when the gain is considerably in excess of my original target.

But there is another feature of this program which is unique. I can decide what price range I want to pay for potential investments. For example, I could tell the computer that I am interested only in shares with current prices ranging between 90p and 200p, or 50p and 500p, or whatever range I choose. The program will trawl through the prices of *all* the shares every time the prices are updated and present me with a list of up to 20 shares which not only fall within my pre-ferred price range, but it will select only those where the price has turned upwards. In other words, it picks shares whose prices have just started to rise thus saving me a lot of time and effort trying to find them myself. It also shows a chart for each one with historic share prices plotted daily over the last two years.

So I have exactly the same information at home that the fund managers have in their offices and I do not have to pay fancy prices for the privilege.

SUMMARY

In this chapter we have described:

- the minimum specifications required to record the necessary data for analysis;
- the amount and type of data to be analysed;
- the importance of recording daily prices of all the shares listed and traded on the stock market.

AREAS FOR INVESTMENT OPPORTUNITIES

INTRODUCTION

In this chapter we look at the areas of the market which are likely to prove to be the best hunting ground for the trader.

There is a widely held credo that penny shares offer a better chance of making money than the more expensive ones. This is untrue. I suppose you can argue that you stand to win more for your bet in a horse or dog race if you back an outsider, and it wins. However, the analogy is false because, in the sporting world, the bookmakers have done their homework before the race starts and *their* opinion as to the chances of each runner beating the others is reflected in the odds on offer. By backing an outsider, the punter is saying that he thinks that *his* judgement of form is better than the market. The bookmakers are frequently wrong in their assessments and it is because of this that the betting game has such an appeal. But although there may appear to be similarities between racing and the stockmarket, they are superficial.

I suppose that you might say that in a horse race you are trying to find the one which will run the distance faster than the others in the same race and to that extent, the study of form (research) will enable you to make a more informed selection and thus increase your chances of winning. However, as far as picking shares is concerned, you are not trying to find the one which will beat all the others. You are trying to find ones which will run faster this time out than they did before, whether they beat the rest or not.

So, in this chapter we shall examine whether it is better to:

- specialise in a sector
- stick to a price range
- use some other method of share selection.

Whatever method you choose for your selection, you will still have to work at collecting as much of the published data so that you are as informed as possible about your choices and their progress. Companies do not stand still. They are fighting to maintain their positions as market leaders or they are striving to increase their share of the market for their goods or services. Maybe they are just plain fighting for survival. Whatever the case may be, they are very similar to an amoeba, constantly changing shape and expanding or contracting. It is the stockmarket opinion (the bookies) which indicates approval or disapproval of what they see and it is this opinion which will generate investor demand or disfavour.

Now, to beat the 'book' you have to have an ability to anticipate an improvement in the market rating of a share. This requires a commitment to regular analyses of company accounts and being quick on your feet. Richard Koch has written a book called *Selecting Shares that Perform* (Pitman Publishing, 128 Long Acre, London WC2E 9AN), and I strongly recommend this as further reading for those who are prepared to do their own analysis in some depth.

SPECIALISING IN A SECTOR

There are many reasons why it can be most useful for a trader to specialise in a sector, particularly for the beginner.

First of all, there is no substitute for experience, and it is not something that you can buy or absorb instantly by reading. Whatever your occupation or absorbing interest has been to date, you will have assimilated enough information to be in a good position to judge the players in the game. You will have more of a 'feel' for the companies involved than you will have for those in other sectors.

Let us suppose that you have never had any interests in commerce, but that you have had an avid interest in politics. Well, you will have experienced the economic results of the different policies between the Labour Party and the Conservatives, particularly as far as their attitudes towards managing the economy is concerned. The most obvious manifestation of the difference between the two political parties is the way in which interest rates have fluctuated. So you could concentrate your research on the way in which the economy is being managed and trying to anticipate whether the base rates are likely to go up or down, or remain static for some time. Thus you would learn all that you can about the effects on gilts

> '... to beat the "book" you have to have an ability to anticipate an improvement in the market rating of a share.'

or other fixed-interest stocks which changes in interest rate might bring, and you would specialise in these investments only.

Whatever sector you choose, you must read as much as you can about the companies which operate in it and try to become an expert in that particular field. Let me give you two examples. The oil sector (see Figure 4.1) on the London Stock Exchange is one in which there are a number of companies of different sizes measured by market capitalisation, but where only two really dominate the rest: these are British Petroleum and Shell.

I shall refer to this table again later on in the book when we come to describing long-term investing, and we shall go through a more detailed examination then. However, as I said at the beginning of this part, the trader is not really interested in what the company does and you might think that I am contradicting myself by suggesting that you get to know as much as possible about a sector. This is not a contradiction because if you are going to specialise in a sector, you really will need to know what makes it tick.

Fig 4.1 Oil companies measured by market capitalisation

(Source: *Sunday Telegraph*)

						P/E
137½	71	Abbot Group	129½*	...	1.8	28.2
42	24½	Aviva	28½	...	–	–
1542	522	Brit Borneo♦*Q*	1325	+40	0.8	56.4
751½	522½	**British Petrl** (p)	751½	+18½	3.2	16.5
3½	1½	Bula Resources	1¾	...	–	–
1167	978	**Burma Cast***Q* (p)	1036½	–3½	5.2	14.0
634½	274	Cairn Energy♦	492½	–24	–	–
26	7½	Dana Pet	21½	...	–	–
4	1	Dragon Oil	3¼	–½	–	–
8	1¼	Emerald Energy	5½	–¼	–	–
701	455	**Enterprise Oil** (p)	700½	–½	3.0	26.9
16½	8¼	Fortune Oil	15¾	+¼	–	63.0
65	39½	Greenway*Q*	39½	–3½	6.3	45.4
330½	234	Hardy Oil	318	+11	0.4	63.6
164½	29¾	JKX Oil	43	+1	–	–
275	172	**Lasmo***Q*	275	+16	e0.5	–
49½	40½	Lasmo 'Ops'	42	...	23.3	–
91¾	56½	Monument♦	91½	+1	–	52.0
159	62	Oil Search	159	+3	–	–
56¾	13½	Pentex Energy	13¾	...	7.9	3.1
60	33¼	Petroz	59	–1	–	–
57½	36½	Pittencrieff	45	...	–	–
45¾	27¾	Premier Oil♦*Q*	45¾	+1¼	1.5	10.3
645	458	Ranger Oil	642½	...	0.6	–
11968¾	9231	Royal Dutch	11968¾	+87	2.6	–
83	47½	Seafield Res	53½	...	–	48.6
1215½	907	**Shell***Q* (p)	1200	+16	3.8	18.9
4117¾	236	Soco Intnl	236	–½	–	–
192	55	Sthn Pacific	185¼	...	–	–
24	11	United Energy	19	...	–	–
538	365	Woodside Pet	508	–2	b0.8	–
23	12½	XCL	14	...	–	–

As I have said, the oil sector is dominated by two large companies. They are BP and Shell. But you really need to start by understanding how the oil business works so that you can put the players into perspective. Here is a bird's eye view of the industry, and a very superficial one, but it will suffice as an example of the way to set about understanding a sector if you should decide to specialise.

The first thing you have to do if you are to become an oil company is to find a source of supply. Almost all the companies in the sector are engaged in searching for oil and this is a very expensive game. For instance, BP spends millions of pounds each year drilling holes in places like Alaska, and Shell does the same in Africa. Both of them are constantly exploring different parts of the world for new productive oil fields. Sometimes this is done alone, sometimes it is carried out in partnership with the countries concerned. This work requires a great deal of capital. Once oil has been found, it has to be extracted, transported to a refinery, processed into saleable fuel, distributed and retailed. Some companies simply spend their time exploring for oil and when they find it, they sell the rights to the product to one of the majors in the industry since they do not have the capital to refine and retail the finished product. Most of the companies listed in the oil sector fall into this category.

I have said that it requires a great deal of capital to carry out exploration drilling, but it requires a great deal more to do all the rest of the transportation and processing required to become a major in this industry. So a third type of operator has emerged. This is a company whose business is in between the exploration wild catter and the major, who exploits the remaining reserves in an oil field when a major has decided that it is no longer economic to continue with the extraction process. Such companies are known as fringe operators. There is one other type of operator who simply acts as an agent by buying and selling oil product from the suppliers. Fortune Oil is an example.

There are many risks attached to trading in oil, but generally they include adequacy of capital resources, currency (exchange rates), political stability in the source countries, interest rates worldwide, and occasionally ethical and environmental considerations.

The PE rating of each share gives you an instant guide to the market's assessment of the risks facing individual companies, and I suggest that you take your benchmark from an average PE of BP and Shell.

If you look at the charts of the more speculative ones, particularly those with a relatively small market capitalisation, you are likely to see the sort of volatility in share price movement which you, as a trader, are seeking. But in view of the risks described above, beware of the number of different factors which can affect a rising price, both adversely and fast.

Isolate each risk and concentrate your reading on those matters which may have a direct bearing on your share selection.

For example, if there is a substantial rise in interest rates, then those companies which have large sums of borrowed money will be hit hardest because they will have to pay more to the lenders. You will find this information from the Extel card.

Figure 4.2 shows an extract from the Extel card for Cairn Energy which is an oil exploration company. You will see that although it has a market capitalisation of £924 million, its pre-tax profit for the year ending 31 December 1996 was only £5.9 million, and yet the borrowings at that date were £28 million, of which £13.6 million are due to be repaid within the next 12 months. The company must be expecting to strike it rich pretty soon, or else it will have to go back to its shareholders and ask for some more permanent capital.

Another consideration is the price of oil. If it drops because the world stocks are too high, then it becomes uneconomic for the fringe operators to continue except at very much reduced levels of activity which in turn will reduce their earnings, and consequently their share price will fall. Such an occurrence is likely to affect all oil share prices across the board, but the ones most at risk will be those with a small market capitalisation.

Political risks are obvious, particularly those which might lead to military or guerrilla action. The majors will be able to survive such contingencies but a smaller exploration company might not. The cost of fire insurance and all the obligatory safety measures which have to be in place nowadays can become so onerous that the smaller compa-

Fig 4.2 Extract from the Extel card for Cairn Energy

(Source: Extel Financial Limited)

| Company Report | COMPANY RESEARCH | May 22, 1997 |

CAIRN ENERGY PLC

Security Name
ORD GBP0.10

Shares in Issue
169,109,009

Latest Dividend
Nett   N/A
Gross   N/A
Tax   N/A
Div Type N/A
Pay Date N/A
Ex Date   N/A

Country of Quotation
United Kingdom

Industrial Classification (SEC)
Oil Exploration and Production

Closing Price
£5.465 down £0.12 (–2%)

Market Capitalisation
£924,180,734

P/E Ratio*
145.35

EPS*
N/A
*Last reported 12 month earnings

Gross Dividend Yield
N/A

Market Codes
SEDOL   0164207
TOPIC   CNE
VALOREN 377070
CUSIP   N/A
TICKER   CNE

NOTE: The information above relates to the security which is deemed to be the company's prime line.

REGISTERED OFFICE
Cairn House, 61 Dublin Street, Edinburgh EH3 6NL Tel: 0131 557 2299 Telex: 727905 Fax: 0131 557 2220/0577

REGISTRARS
Bank of Scotland, Registrar Department, Apex House, 9 Haddington Place, Edinburgh EH7 4AL Scotland Tel: 0131 243 5366 Fax: 0131 243 5327

DIRECTORS
NON EXECUTIVE CHAIRMAN: N. Lessels CBE
EXECUTIVE DEPUTY CHAIRMAN: H.M. Grossart
CHIEF EXECUTIVE: W.B.B. Gammell
FINANCE: Agnes Macleod
EXECUTIVE: P.O.J. Tracy BSc MSc CEng
NON EXECUTIVE: Sir David Thomson Bt; P.J. Fowler CMG

SECRETARY
H.R. Dundas MA CA

BANKERS
Bank of Scotland

MERCHANT BANKERS
Deutsche Morgan Grenfell & Co Ltd

AUDITORS
Ernst & Young

BROKERS
Societe Generale Strauss Turnbull Securities Ltd

SOLICITORS
Shepherd & Wedderburn, WS

COMPANY HISTORY
Incorporated on 14-04-1971; Registered No Sc48610; Re-registered 20-05-1981 as a Public Limited Company under the Companies Act, 1980 The name changed on 27-04-1971 from Offshore Exploration Scotland Ltd to Caledonian Offshore Company Ltd and on 25-04-1988 to Cairn Energy PLC. On 22-12-1988 the Company's Ordinary shares of £1 were introduced to the Stock Exchange.

ACTIVITIES
The principal activity of the Group is the exploration for and production of oil and gas in the United Kingdom and internationally.

SUBSIDIARIES
PRINCIPAL. EXPLORATION AND PRODUCTION: Cairn Energy Onshore Ltd; Cairn Energy Far East Ltd (Hong Kong, Operating in Thailand); Holland Sea Search Holding NV (Netherlands); Command Petroleum Ltd (Australia, Operating in India); Cairn Petroleum Ltd (Australia); Cairn Energy Thailand Ltd (Thailand); C.E. North America Inc (USA); Holland Sea Search Bangladesh BV (Netherlands, Operating in Bangladesh); Holland Sea Search BV (Netherlands); Holland Sea Search II BV (Netherlands); Holland Sea Search Inc (USA, Operating in the Netherlands) HOLDING COMPANIES: Cairn Energy Holdings Ltd; Cairn Energy Australia Pty Ltd; Cairn Energy Group Holdings BV (Netherlands)

CAIRN ENERGY PLC

ASSOCIATED COMPANIES

PRINCIPAL. EXPLORATION & PRODUCTION: Comeco Petroleum Inc (41.2%, USA, Operating in Yemen); SOCO Perm Russia Inc (21.2%, USA, Operating in Russia)

CAPITAL at 31-12-96

	AUTHORISED	ISSUED	SHARES ISSUED
Ordinary shares of 10p	£22,500,000	£16,899,000	168,990,000

CAPITAL HISTORY

1989	May	6,346,050 Ord	Part funding of consideration for oil and gas properties of Lignum Oil Co all of which subject to Open Offer – 5.9 at 220p (Cum price 220p; xe 13-04-89)
1990	Apr	5,330,560 Ord	Rights – 3:10 at 265; (Cum price 320p; xr 06-04-90)
	Dec	1,215,763 Ord	Consideration for 22.22% interest in CEP Vietnam (Blocks 17 & 21) SA
1992	May	–	Subdivision – £1 Ord to 10p Ord and 90p Defd
	Oct	24,315,263 Ord all of which are subject to Open Offer	Placing at 27p per share – 1:1 at 27p (cum price 32p; xe 08-10-92)
1993	Apr	12,157,631 Ord all of which are subject to Open Offer	Placing at 43p per share – 1:4 at 43p (Cum price 45p; xe 08-04-93)
	May	1,166,666 Ord	Placing at 62p per share
	May	2,831,347 Ord	Consideration for acquisition of Teredo
	Jul	1 Ord	Acquisition of 24,315,263 Defd shares
	Jul	(24,315,263) Defd	Redeemed
1995	Jul	94,542 Ord	Consideration for HSSH
	Aug	21,847,036 Ord	Rights – 1:3 at 80p (Cum price 86p; xr 27-07-95)
	Dec	164,000 Ord	Options
	Dec	4,377,703 Ord	Issued at 111.5p
1996	Aug	18,421,796 Ord	Rights – 1:5 at 280p (Cum price 318p; xr 26-07-96)
	Dec	19,468,328 Ord	Conversion of loan stock (Issued by way of Rights – 19:108 at 190p (Cum price 373.5p; xr 21-10-96))
	Dec	31,957,846 Ord	Consideration for Command Petroleum Ltd
		475,500 Ord	Options

ACQUISITION HISTORY

1991	Jan		Eastern Espana SA
1992	Feb	US$1.5m cash	64% interest in Omni Exploration Inc
	Oct		Licence interest from ARCO British Ltd
1993	May	2,831,347 Ord	Teredo Petroleum PLC
1995	Dec	£17.2m case & 756,866 Ord	HSSH
	Aug	£16.0m cash	Clyde Petroleum (North Sea) Ltd
1996	Dec	£41.3m cash & 38,859,209 Ord	Command Petroleum Ltd

RIGHTS OF SHARES

VOTING: One vote per share

WARRANT RIGHTS

The Company has issued warrants to subscribe for Ordinary shares. The warrant holder can subscribe for 640,000 Ordinary shares at a price of £2.355 per share. The warrants are exercisable in whole or in part in a five year period beginning on 01-04-93.

SHAREHOLDINGS

DIRECTORS' INTERESTS in the Ordinary shares of the Company at 14-03-97:
BENEFICIAL: 675,353. OPTIONS: 1,673,000.
MAJOR SHAREHOLDERS in the shares of the Company at 14-03-97: Mercury Asset Management PLC 21,720,195 (12.85%); Robert Fleming Holdings Ltd 12,895,604 (7.63%); SOCO International Inc 11,731,994 (6.94%); Gartmore Investment Management Ltd 6,099,603 (3.61%); Standard Life Group 5,322,829 (3.15%).

CAIRN ENERGY PLC

DIVIDEND PAYMENT DETAILS –
ORDINARY Year end December 31

None yet paid.

PER SHARE RECORD OF 10p ORDINARY –
Adjusted for Capital Changes

	Dec 31 1992	Dec 31 1993	Dec 31 1994	Dec 31 1995	Dec 31 1996
EARNINGS (LOSS) based on Reported Profits					
Basic – Under FRS 3	2.96p	3.44p	7.68p	11.70p	3.12p
EARNINGS (LOSS) based on Adjusted Profits					
IIMR Headline	2.71p	1.63p	0.83p	1.86p	3.76p
Shares on which earnings calculated (000's)					
Basic	a28,235	a58,972	a64,786	a75,524	a104,027
NET DIVIDEND	–	–	–	–	–
DIVIDEND COVER	–	–	–	–	–
NET ASSET VALUE					
At B/s date	50.8p	49.9p	57.1p	68.7p	188.4p
Capital Issue Factor (a)Weighted average	0.991	–	0.983	0.908	–

PRICES to December 31 – Adjusted for Capital Changes

LONDON

ORDINARY (pence)	1992	1993	1994	1995	1996
High	67.5	61.4	78.1	106.2	417.0
Low	18.9	28.8	50.9	65.8	106.2

BORROWINGS at 31-12-96

LOANS
8% CONVERTIBLE DEBENTURE 1988. Outstanding: £1,192,000. (£596,000 due within one year). The loan is repayable at par in five equal instalments on July 1 each year up to and including 1998. Interest is charged at a fixed rate of 8% per annum.
BANK LOANS
Outstanding: £28,117,000. (£13,663,000 due within one year). Denominated in US Dollars and Netherland Guilders.

CONSENSUS FORECAST

Forecast last revised February 23, 1996

			a Dec 1994	Dec 1995	Dec 1996
Pre Tax Profit	(£m)	LATEST	1.20	–	–
		High		–	–
		Low	–	–	
		Previous		4.00	3.41
		Std. Deviation		–	–
EPS	(Pence)	LATEST	1.80	5.50	5.10
		High		5.50	5.10
		Low		5.50	5.10
		Previous		6.20	5.30
		Std. Deviation		–	–
EPS Growth		LATEST		511.10	(7.30)
		Previous		244.40	(14.50)
Dividend	(Pence)	LATEST	1.00	–	–
		High		–	–
		Low		–	–
		Previous		–	–
		Std. Deviation		–	–
No of brokers		LATEST		1	1
		Previous		0	0

(a) Actual figures.

Consensus estimates and actuals provided by FIRST CALL INTERNATIONAL

Copyright 1996
Telephone 0171-825-8888 – Fax 0171-608-3514
No responsibility accepted for error or omission
Extel is part of Financial Times Information

Company Report	COMPANY RESEARCH	May 22, 1997

CAIRN ENERGY PLC

INTERIM RESULTS
Consolidated Interim Results for 6 months (Unaudited)

Profit & Loss Account

	Jun 30 1995 £000s	Jun 30 1996 £000s	
TURNOVER	5,153.0	16,935.0	+228.6
REP OPERATING PROF (LOSS)	174.0	3,381.0	+1,843.1
Interest income	436.0	174.0	−60.1
Interest payable	(260.0)	(1,046.0)	+302.3
FA disposal gain (loss)	9,488.0	−	n/a
Fixed assets w/o	(1,050.0)	−	n/a
Business disp gain (loss)	(793.0)	−	n/a
PROFIT (LOSS) BEFORE TAX	7,995.0	2,509.0	−68.6
Tax	(2,900.0)	−	n/a
PROFIT (LOSS) AFTER TAX	5,095.0	2,509.0	−50.8
Reported EPS (p)	7.72000	2.73000	−64.6
Reported adjusted EPS (p)	0.53000	2.73000	+415.1

Balance Sheet

	Jun 30 1995 £000s	Jun 30 1996 £000s	
Tangible assets	49,518.0	100,951.0	+103.9
Financial assets	1,890.0	1,758.0	−7.0
FIXED ASSETS	51,408.0	102,709.0	+99.8
Debtors	8,939.0	9,462.0	+5.9
Cash & equivalents	20,444.0	3,194.0	−84.4
CURRENT ASSETS	29,383.0	12,656.0	−56.9
TOTAL ASSETS	80,791.0	115,365.0	+42.8
CREDS DUE WITHIN 1 YEAR	18,780.0	19,586.0	+4.3
NET CURR ASSETS (LIABS)	10,603.0	(6,930.0)	n/a
ASSETS LESS CURR LIABS	62,011.0	95,779.0	+54.5
Other long term liabs	14,508.0	21,177.0	+46.0
Provisions	1,358.0	3,444.0	+153.6
NET ASSETS (LIABS)	46,145.0	71,158.0	+54.2
SHARE CAPITAL	6,545.0	9,193.0	+40.5
RESERVES	37,412.0	61,965.0	+65.6
SHAREHOLDERS' FUNDS	43,957.0	71,158.0	+61.9
Minorities	2,188.0	−	n/a

CONSOLIDATED PROFIT AND LOSS ACCOUNT

	Dec 31 1992 £000	Dec 31 1993 £000	Dec 31 1994 £000	Dec 31 1995 £000	Dec 31 1996 £000
TURNOVER	13,090	18,181	15,589	21,747	36,460
Cost of sales	(9,954)	(13,553)	(12,690)	(17,974)	(23,764)
GROSS PROFIT	3,136	4,628	2,899	3,773	12,696
Administration exps	(1,758)	2,064	(1,848)	(1,707)	(4,730)
Write-down of assets	−	(2,657)	(4,724)	−	−
Misc other tdg inc	58	34	−	−	−
Exceptional chgs-tdg	−	−	−	(1,050)	(661)
TRADING PROFIT (LOSS)	1,436	(59)	(3,673)	1,016	7,305
Interest income	148	194	433	716	1,221
Interest payable	(1,308)	(985)	(801)	(1,381)	(1,865)
Other (exp) inc net	542	(504)	103	148	(734)
Exceptional profits	−	3,659	13,329	8,964	−
PROFIT BEFORE TAX	818	2,305	9,391	9,463	5,927
Tax	−	−	(4,100)	(575)	(2,681)
PROFIT AFTER TAX	818	2,305	5,291	8,888	3,246
Minority interests	37	(232)	(198)	1	−
NET INCOME	855	2,073	5,093	8,889	3,246
Ordinary dividends	−	−	−	−	−
RETAINED PROFITS	855	2,073	5,093	8,889	3,246

CAIRN ENERGY PLC

NOTES TO CONSOLIDATED PROFIT AND LOSS ACCOUNT

	Dec 31 1992 £000	Dec 31 1993 £000	Dec 31 1994 £000	Dec 31 1995 £000	Dec 31 1996 £000
EXCEPTIONAL CHGS-TDG					
Fixed assets w/o-tdg	–	–	–	(1,050)	(661)
INTEREST PAYABLE					
Int within 5 yrs	(1,129)	(978)	(801)	(1,287)	(1,726)
Int on finance leases	(179)	(7)	–	(94)	(139)
	(1,308)	(985)	(801)	(1,381)	(1,865)
EXCEPTIONAL PROFITS					
FA disposal gain	–	–	–	9,488	–
Business disps gain	–	3,659	13,329	(524)	–
	–	3,659	13,329	8,964	–
TAX BY COUNTRY					
Corporation tax	–	–	(2,400)	–	–
Domestic deferred tax	–	–	–	–	(2,000)
Domestic tax	–	–	(2,400)	–	(2,000)
Overseas tax	–	–	(1,700)	(575)	(681)
	–	–	(4,100)	(575)	(2,681)
TAX BY TYPE					
Current taxation	–	–	(4,100)	(3,030)	61
Deferred taxation	–	–	–	–	(2,742)
Prior years tax	–	–	–	2,455	–
	–	–	(4,100)	(575)	(2,681)
TAX					
Tax on exceptionals	–	–	(4,100)	(575)	–
RETAINED PROFITS					
Parent company	(535)	1,910	12,305	9,091	(763)
Subsidiaries	1,390	163	(7,212)	(202)	4,009
	855	2,073	5,093	8,889	3,246
PROFIT BEFORE TAX is after (charging) crediting					
Directors emoluments	(376)	(443)	(409)	(569)	(1,873)
Ex gratia payments	–	(50)	(100)	–	–
Wages & salaries	(1,465)	(1,825)	(2,513)	(2,698)	(5,568)
Social security	(137)	(165)	(272)	(275)	(447)
Staff pensions	(152)	(159)	(225)	(231)	(305)
Staff expenses	(1,754)	(2,149)	(3,010)	(3,204)	(6,320)
Auditors remuneration	(46)	(68)	(37)	(53)	(98)
Non-audit fees	(31)	(188)	(102)	(133)	(42)
Optg lease rentals	(301)	(320)	(350)	(287)	(336)
Depreciation	(264)	(245)	(177)	(176)	(394)
Net forex gn (loss)	548	(120)	261	235	(600)
Rental income net	86	32	44	136	90
Fixed assets w/o	–	(2,657)	(4,724)	–	–
Av no of staff	56	58	81	103	145

CAIRN ENERGY PLC

Additional notes to CONSOLIDATED PROFIT AND LOSS ACCOUNT

	Dec 31 1992 £000	Dec 31 1993 £000	Dec 31 1994 £000	Dec 31 1995 £000	Dec 31 1996 £000
OPTG LEASE RENTALS					
Land & buildings	(292)	(298)	(334)	(287)	(336)
Other	(9)	(22)	(16)	–	–
	(301)	(320)	(350)	(287)	(336)
DEPRECIATION					
Owned assets	(212)	(193)	(171)	(175)	(394)
Leased assets	(52)	(52)	(6)	(1)	–
	(264)	(245)	(177)	(176)	(394)

CONSOLIDATED PROFIT AND LOSS ACCOUNT – Continuing

	Dec 31 1994 £000	Dec 31 1995 £000	Dec 31 1996 £000
TURNOVER	9,041	21,747	36,460
Cost of sales	(8150)	(17,974)	(23,764)
GROSS PROFIT	891	3,773	12,696
Administration exps	(975)	(1,707)	(4,730)
Net other tdg exps	(4,724)	(1,050)	(661)
TDG PROFIT (LOSS)	(4,808)	1,016	7,305
EXCPL PROFITS			
Profit on disposal	13,329	9,488	–
Business disps gain	–	(524)	–
	13,329	8,964	–

CONSOLIDATED PROFIT AND LOSS ACCOUNT
Continuing – Acquired

	Dec 31 1994 £000	Dec 31 1995 £000	Dec 31 1996 £000
TURNOVER	–	11,152	2,861
Cost of sales	–	(8,847)	(1,631)
GROSS PROFIT	–	2,305	1,230
Administration exps	–	(535)	(190)
TRADING PROFIT	–	1,770	1,040

CONSOLIDATED PROFIT AND LOSS ACCOUNT
Discontinued

	Dec 31 1994 £000	Dec 31 1995 £000	Dec 31 1996 £000
TURNOVER	6,548	–	–
Cost of sales	(4,540)	–	–
GROSS PROFIT	2,008	–	–
Administration exps	(873)	–	–
TRADING PROFIT	1,135	–	–

GEOGRAPHICAL ANALYSIS – Turnover by source

	Dec 31 1992 £000	Dec 31 1993 £000	Dec 31 1994 £000	Dec 31 1995 £000	Dec 31 1996 £000
UK	a	7,544	9,041	17,839	24,589
Europe	4,964	1,359	1,661	3,779	8,715
USA	7,952	8,981	4,887	–	–
International	174	297	–	129	3,156
	13,090	18,181	15,589	21,747	36,460

a) Not shown separately.

CAIRN ENERGY PLC

GEOGRAPHICAL ANALYSIS – Profit by source

	Dec 31 1992 £000	Dec 31 1993 £000	Dec 31 1994 £000	Dec 31 1995 £000	Dec 31 1996 £000
UK	a	(2,324)	(4,808)	854	5,338
Rest of Europe	–	287	166	–	–
Europe	(471)	–	–	182	1,611
USA	1,907	2,047	969	–	(661)
International	–	(69)	–	(20)	1,017
Exceptional chge	–	3,659	13,329	8,964	–
Net interest exp	(618)	(1,295)	(265)	(517)	(1,378)
	818	2,305	9,391	9,463	5,927

a) Not shown separately.

CONSOLIDATED STATEMENT OF CASH FLOWS

	Dec 31 1992 £000	Dec 31 1993 £000	Dec 31 1994 £000	Dec 31 1995 £000	Dec 31 1996 £000
OPERATING ACTIVITIES	6,531	9,480	8,416	8,990	16,779
INVESTMENT RETURN AND SERVICING OF FINANCE					
Interest received	141	181	405	701	1,111
Interest paid	(1,378)	(1,395)	(993)	(1,379)	(2,088)
	(1,237)	(1,214)	(588)	(678)	(977)
TAXATION	–	–	–	(4,545)	61
INVESTING ACTIVITIES					
Subsidiaries acqd	(724)	(267)	–	(31,536)	(43,596)
Tangibles acquired	(8,436)	(13,013)	(22,652)	(13,727)	(33,607)
Subsidiaries sold	–	1,287	20,132	2,089	–
Investments sold	–	111	230	16,584	–
Tangibles sold	34	841	2,069	11	1,233
Shares in sub issued	–	11,537	–	–	–
	(9,126)	496	(221)	(26,579)	(75,970)
NET CASH FLOW BEFORE FINANCING	(3,832)	8,762	7,607	(22,812)	(60,107)
FINANCING					
Long term debt raised	–	–	5,801	–	76,488
Share capital issued	6,566	5,951	–	17,522	57,100
Long term debt repaid	(1,060)	(11,975)	–	(7,344)	(12,426)
Finance leases repaid	(38)	(62)	(10)	–	–
Issue expenses	(490)	(268)	–	(585)	(4,976)
Misc financing inflow	–	–	–	–	(57,190)
	4,978	(6,354)	5,791	9,593	58,996
CASH INCR (DECR)	1,146	2,408	13,398	(13,219)	(1,111)
Currency appreciation	–	–	374	–	–
B/S CASH INCR (DECR)	1,146	2,408	13,772	(13,219)	(1,111)

NOTES TO CONSOLIDATED STATEMENT OF CASH FLOWS

	Dec 31 1992 £000	Dec 31 1993 £000	Dec 31 1994 £000	Dec 31 1995 £000	Dec 31 1996 £000
OPERATING ACTIVITIES					
Trading profit (loss)	1,436	(59)	(3,673)	1,016	7,305
Depletion & depn	4,661	8,862	10,850	10,081	13,450
Abandonment provn	149	364	420	516	707
Other tdg adj incr	1,005	(112)	615	196	(1,741)
Decrease in debtors	142	1,051	(2,693)	(3,667)	1,034
Increase in creditors	(862)	(650)	2,913	848	(3,976)
C/A invest movement	–	24	(16)	–	–
	6,531	9,480	8,416	8,990	16,779
CASH INCR (DECR)					
Cash & near cash	–	–	–	(13,219)	(1,111)

Company Report	COMPANY RESEARCH	May 22, 1997

CAIRN ENERGY PLC

CONSOLIDATED BALANCE SHEETS

	Dec 31 1992 £000	Dec 31 1993 £000	Dec 31 1994 £000	Dec 31 1995 £000	Dec 31 1996 £000
FIXED ASSETS					
Tangible assets	44,153	52,288	27,386	94,872	262,656
Financial assets	142	–	7,096	1,873	22,746
	44,295	52,288	34,482	96,745	285,402
CURRENT ASSETS					
Trade debtors	2,307	3,102	3,029	5,908	8,523
Prepays/accrued inc	465	596	1,938	8,336	4,522
Other debtors	523	2,736	976	2,281	10,537
Cash & equivalents	2,113	4,359	16,709	3,490	65,305
Listed investments	–	214	–	–	–
	5,408	11,007	22,652	20,015	88,887
CREDS due within 1 yr					
Short term debt	2,893	1,948	2,933	5,997	14,259
Pble-group cos	–	–	–	–	1,483
Trade creditors	562	897	517	8,525	4,198
Accruals	1,167	1,780	3,243	2,475	11,727
Revenue tax	–	–	4,100	130	130
Tax & social security	48	49	101	397	794
Other taxation	1,446	68	48	550	1,696
	6,116	4,742	10,942	18,074	34,287
NET CURR ASSETS (LIAB)	(708)	6,265	11,710	1,941	54,600
TOTAL ASSETS LESS CURRENT LIABILITIES	43,587	58,553	46,192	98,686	340,002
CREDS due after 1 yr					
Long term debt	14,362	10,777	2,983	25,528	15,110
Other L/T Creditors	–	–	–	–	405
	14,362	10,777	2,983	25,528	15,515
PROVISIONS	643	1,325	1,747	3,169	6,127
NET ASSETS	28,582	46,451	41,462	69,989	318,360
SHARE CAPITAL	26,747	6,479	6,479	9,193	16,899
Share premium	24,513	28,863	6,881	26,659	180,575
Capital reserves	2,499	2,470	24,678	21,008	116,279
Profit & loss account	(25,867)	(23,385)	3,424	12,749	4,607
Cap redemption res	–	21,884	–	–	–
SHAREHOLDERS' FUNDS	27,892	36,311	41,462	69,609	318,360
Minority interests	690	10,140	–	380	–
NET ASSETS	28,582	46,451	41,462	69,989	318,360

NOTES TO CONSOLIDATED BALANCE SHEETS

	Dec 31 1992 £000	Dec 31 1993 £000	Dec 31 1994 £000	Dec 31 1995 £000	Dec 31 1996 £000
TANGIBLE ASSETS					
F/H property-cost	80	–	–	–	746
F/H prop depn	(9)	–	–	–	–
Freehold property NBV	71	–	–	–	746
Oil & gas prop – cost	94,202	112,001	62,028	138,763	312,556
Oil & gas prop – depn	(50,474)	(60,129)	(34,981)	(44,300)	(51,665)
Oil & gas prop NBV	43,728	51,872	27,047	94,463	260,891
Oth tangible FA–cost	1,097	1,349	1,145	1,380	2,330
Oth tangible FA depn	(743)	(933)	(806)	(971)	(1,311)
Other tangible FA NBV	354	416	339	409	1,019
Tangible assets	44,153	52,288	27,386	94,872	262,656

CAIRN ENERGY PLC

FINANCIAL ASSETS					
Listed investments	142	–	7,096	–	–
Unlisted investments	–	–	–	1,873	22,746
Investments	142	–	7,096	1,873	22,746
LISTED INVESTMENTS					
Notes etc-mkt valn	–	187	–	–	–
DEBTORS includes					
Due after one year	213	422	–	–	–
DEBT BY TYPE					
Loan stock	480	–	–	2,125	1,192
Bank loans	16,541	12,715	5,916	29,400	28,177
Finance leases & HP	72	10	–	–	–
Bank overdraft	162	–	–	–	–
	17,255	12,725	5,916	31,525	29,369
DEBT BY MATURITY					
Short term loans	162	–	–	–	–
Current maturities	2,731	1,948	2,933	5,997	14,259
Short term debt	2,893	1,948	2,933	5,997	14,259
Due within 1 to 2 yrs	5,830	6,145	2,983	8,520	6,329
Due within 2 to 5 yrs	8,520	4,632	–	17,008	8,781
Due after 1 year	12	–	–	–	–
	17,255	12,725	5,916	31,525	29,369
DEBT BY SECURITY					
Secured	16,613	12,725	5,916	31,525	29,369
Unsecured	642	–	–	–	–
	17,255	12,725	5,916	31,525	29,369
PROVISIONS					
Deferred taxation	–	–	–	–	3,247
Provisions	643	1,325	1,747	3,169	2,780
	643	1,325	1,747	3,169	6,127
SHARE CAPITAL					
Ordinary shares	4,863	6,479	6,479	9,193	16,899
Deferred shares	21,884	–	–	–	–
	26,747	6,479	6,479	9,193	16,899
COMMITMENTS AND CONTINGENCIES					
Capital contracted	888	565	1,530	9,102	59,246
Cap not contracted	2,611	14,515	7,300	12,612	–
Optg leases-property	298	341	298	320	750
Exploration commits	–	–	4,500	–	–

CHAIRMAN'S STATEMENT

The current year has started with the same sense of optimism as last year. Production and cash inflows are set to increase, and exploration and development activity will be intense. To supplement this, and to seek further gain for shareholders, we shall pursue new ventures, strategic alliances and, where appropriate, acquisitions. We enter 1997, therefore, with the real prospect of substantial further growth backed up by a committed and focused management team equipped and determined to deliver it.

ANNUAL GENERAL MEETING (year to 31-12-96)

Cairn House, 61 Dublin Street, Edinburgth EH3 6NL, May 6 at 12.30pm.

FINANCIAL CALENDAR

Interim Report 29th August 1996; Preliminary Figures 19th March 1997; Annual General Meeting 6th May 1997.

nies are finding it less and less viable economically to undertake much exploration work in deep sea areas.

So, to become an expert you should have a checklist which reduces your research to the essential items for you to check *before* you buy. Also, when you become conversant with the headings, you will become alert subconsciously to any item of news which might have a bearing on your chosen sector. Perhaps you might include the following items.

- **Market capitalisation**. Establish the market leaders. Available from the *Financial Times*.
- **PE benchmark**. Use an average of the market leaders.
- **Give a rating to the risks**. 1 = Low; 10 = High
- **Borrowings as a percentage of shareholders funds**. Use an average of the market leaders. Available from the Extel card, but you will have to make your own calculations.
- **Interest rates**. How much of an adverse effect a rise will have.
- **Currency**. Are the company's markets preponderantly in stable currency areas or places like South America or newly emerged African states?
- **Political**. Is there a risk from UK or European or American politics, let alone other more unstable or unpredictable governments? Divide this risk, if necessary, between sources of product or raw material on one hand, and markets for the finished goods on the other.
- **Product life**. For example, computer technology or pharmaceutical drug development can have an extremely limited life.
- **Competition**. New products, particularly from countries with cheap labour costs.
- **Advertising**. Is there a lot of it and is it mostly Press or TV? Is it being sustained?

This may seem a bit daunting at first sight, but a little practice will enable you to make your judgements very fast and without spending much time on your reading. Most of it is commonsense anyway, and will come to you in the normal course of following current affairs.

STICKING TO A PRICE RANGE

There are a great many people who select their shares simply by refusing to buy what they term as 'heavy weight' or expensive shares. There is nothing wrong with this practice, but it often means that they miss out on some good profits.

> **The most important thing to remember is that it is the *percentage profit* that counts, and nothing else.**

By sticking to a low price range, you are asking for the share price to grow by a large percentage if your target profit is to be achieved.

Let us take an example.

■ **EXAMPLE: United Energy**

The first thing to look at on the chart over the last 12 months are the highs and lows of the share price (see Figure 4.3).

The low was almost out of sight, and the high was 24p early in 1997.

The share price pattern has established a new trading range since February after a sustained rise from August 1996.

The immediate conclusions to be drawn are as follows:

(a) The spread of the share price – 20p bid, 23p offered – is large. It amounts to 15 per cent which is ridiculous when you look at the spreads of the quality shares in the FTSE 100. For example, in the same week that I obtained this data, Shell was standing at 1026p bid, 1027p offered. A spread of 1p or 0.09 per cent. So the price of United Energy would have to move up *at least* 15 per cent before you break even, and that is *before* you take dealing costs and stamp duty into consideration.

(b) Now would not be the time to buy the share anyway, because it is standing in the wrong part of its trading range. It is definitely in the 'over-bought' area of the trading range.

(c) If the share price continues to follow its recent pattern, whilst there is good volatility, the trading range oscillates between about 19p and 22p. This represents a bottom-to-top variation of 3p on 19p, or 15.78 per cent. The

Fig 4.3 United Energy: share price mid-July to mid-June 1997

(Source: Topic)

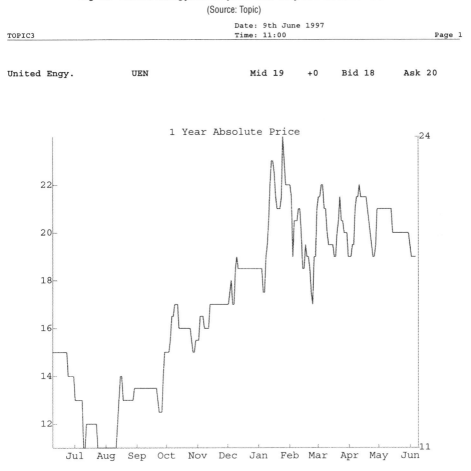

chart prices are mid-prices so you will still have the spreads to take into consideration as well as dealing costs.

(d) There is an interesting configuration which occurred in March/early April. You will note the existence of a double bottom on the chart at that time, which has been followed by a rise in the share price as you would expect. Nevertheless, unless the price breaks through the upper level of the trading range, you would expect the next movement to be downwards.

Now, although this should *not* be a share which you should be considering adding to your holding at the current price, it will be a worthwhile exercise to look at the Extel card and extract the few essential statistics (see Figure 4.4).

Fig 4.4 Extract from the Extel card for United Energy

(Source: Extel Financial Limited)

Company Report	COMPANY RESEARCH	April 3, 1997

UNITED ENERGY PLC

Security Name
ORD 10P

Shares in Issue
38,791,895

Latest Dividend

Nett	0p
Gross	N/A
Tax	N/A
Div Type	Interim dividend
Pay Date	October 1996
Ex Date	October 1996

Country of Quotation
United Kingdom

Industrial Classification (SEC)
Oil Exploration and Production

Closing Price
£0.19 (No change)

Market Capitalisation
£7,370,460

P/E Ratio*
54.29

EPS*
N/A

*Last reported 12 month earnings

Gross Dividend Yield
0%

Market Codes

SEDOL	0917285
TOPIC	UEN
VALOREN	N/A
CUSIP	N/A
TICKER	UEN

NOTE: The information above relates to the security which is deemed to be the company's prime line.

REGISTERED OFFICE
50 Stratton Street, London W1X 6NX Tel: 0171 493 9933 Fax: 0171 629 7900

REGISTRARS
Independent Registrars Group Ltd, Balfour House, 390-398 High Road, Ilford, Essex IG1 1NQ
England Tel: 0181 478 8241 Fax: 0181 478 7717

DIRECTORS
NON EXECUTIVE CHAIRMAN: J. F. Billington
CHIEF EXECUTIVE AND FINANCE: N. J. Tamblyn ACA
EXECUTIVE: D. Howard-Orchard; J. A. Hoskinson (Ceased 31-03-97)
NON EXECUTIVE: A. B. Haywood (Ceased 31-12-96); J. A. Hoskinson (Appointed 01-04-97)

SECRETARY
J. A. Hoskinson

PRINCIPAL BANKERS
Bank One; Lloyds Bank PLC

AUDITORS
KPMG

BROKERS
Peel, Hunt & Co Ltd; John Siddall & Son Ltd

FINANCIAL ADVISERS
Henry Ansbacher & Co Ltd

SOLICITORS
Nabarro Nathanson

COMPANY HISTORY
Incorporated on 05-04-1983 as a Private Company; Registered No 1712354; Re-registered on
25-05-1983 as a Public Limited Company under The Companies Act, 1980. The name changed
on 25-05-1983 from Shelfco (No.12) Ltd to Falcon Resources PLC and on 13-08-1990 to
United Energy PLC. In July 1984, 10,325,735 Ordinary shares of 20p were introduced to The
Stock Exchange. The listing was cancelled on 13-08-90, and on the same date following a
capital reorganisation, 242,970,460 Ordinary shares of 1p were introduced to the Stock
Exchange Unlisted Securities Market.

ACTIVITIES
The principal activities of the Group are the development and production of proved and near
proved oil and gas reserves in the USA and electricity generation from waste products in the
UK.

SUBSIDIARIES
PRINCIPAL: HOLDING COMPANY: AmBrit International PLC
DIRECT INVESTMENT IN OIL AND GAS PROPERTIES: AmBrit Resources Ltd; AmBrit Energy
Corp (USA)
POST YEAR END ACQUISITIONS: Agrigen Ltd (30.0% - Acquired 29-01-96); Ham Gossett Oil
Field (74.8%, USA - acquired 10-04-96); Mullin Lease (Acquired 04-11-96)

UNITED ENERGY PLC

CAPITAL at 31-12-95

	AUTHORISED	ISSUED	SHARES ISSUED
Ordinary shares of 10p	£5,500,000	£3,705,257	37,052,568

CAPITAL HISTORY

1990	Aug	–	Subdivision – 10p Ord to 1p Ord and 9p Defd
	Aug	37,500,000 Ord	Issued to Venturelarge Ltd in part consideration for indebtedness
	Aug	17,500,000 Ord	Consideration for indebtedness of The Blue Grass Corporation
	Aug	6,536,361 Ord	Part consideration for further 46.4% interest in Falcon-Andrau Energy Co 1984 Drilling Programme No 1
	Aug	141,277,845 Ord	Rights – 3:1 at 2p (xr 13-08-90)
1991	Jul	31,340 Ord	Warrants
	Oct	(46,692,615) Defd	Cancelled
	Oct	–	Reduction by 0.5p to 0.5p Ord
	Oct	–	Consolidation – 0.5p Ord to 10p Ord
1992	Feb	21,173,214 Ord	Part consideration for AmBrit International PLC
		11,237 Ord	Warrants
1994		15 Ord	Warrants
1995	Mar	3,389,785 Ord	Part consideration for Renown oil and gas properties
		3 Ord	Warrants

ACQUISITION HISTORY

1992	Feb	21,173,214 Ord plus £46,000 cash	AmBrit International PLC
	Jun	US$1.35m cash	25% working interest in two properties: Johnson & James Fields, Foard & Young Counties, Texas
1993	Jun	US$610,000 cash	Hilliard group of properties
1995	Mar	3,389,785 Ord plus US$3.01m cash	Oil and gas properties from Renown Petroleum Inc

RIGHTS OF SHARES

VOTING: One vote per share

WARRANT RIGHTS

At 31-12-95, there were 1,838,745 warrants outstanding to subscribe for Ordinary shares of 10p at 40p per share during the subscription periods ending on or before 11-02-96.

OPTION AGREEMENTS

Two ex-directors, Messrs J.M.V. Butterfield and A.P.O. Alderton, are intersted in options to acquire Ordinary shares in the Company.

SHAREHOLDINGS

DIRECTORS' INTERESTS in the Ordinary shares of the Company at 29-04-96; BENEFICIAL: J.F. Billington 7,512,461; Others 649,574. NON BENEFICIAL: Others 198,750. WARRANTS: 910,824 Beneficial; 24,444 Non Beneficial.
OPTIONS: 2,719,328.
MAJOR SHAREHOLDERS in the Company at 29-04-96: Renown Petroleum Inc 2,079,633 (5.36%); Ansbacher Nominees Ltd 2,025,460 (5.22%); West Ashby Investments Ltd 1,846,263 (4.76%); State Street Nominees Ltd JD38 1,486,270 (3.83%); Cut-Off Investments LP 1,310,152 (3.38%).

DIVIDEND PAYMENT DETAILS –

ORDINARY Year end December 31

None yet paid

UNITED ENERGY PLC

PER SHARE RECORD OF 10p ORDINARY –
Adjusted for Capital Changes

	Dec 31 1991	Dec 31 1992	Dec 31 1993	Dec 31 1994	Dec 31 1995
EARNINGS (LOSS) based on Reported Profits					
Basic	(1.00p)	0.20p	0.10p	(1.10p)	0.30p
EARNINGS (LOSS) based on Adjusted Profits					
IIMR Headline	(1.02p)	0.19p	0.07p	(1.05p)	0.31p
Shares on which earnings calculated (000's)					
Basic	a12,476	a30,378	a33,662	a33,663	a35,446
NET DIVIDEND	–	–	–	–	–
DIVIDEND COVER	–	–	–	–	–
NET ASSET VALUE					
At B/s date	9.1p	15.5p	15.2p	13.9p	14.0p
Capital Issue Factor	–	–	–	–	–

(a) Weighted average.

PRICES to December 31 – Adjusted for Capital Changes

LONDON

ORDINARY (pence)	1991	1992	1993	1994	1995
High	62.0	41.0	28.0	23.0	14.0
Low	21.0	11.0	14.0	13.0	8.0

BORROWINGS at 31-12-95

BANK LOAN
Outstanding: £4,477,000. Repayable by 31-12-1999. Interest is payable at a rate of 1/2% above US Prime Rate.

INTERIM RESULTS

Consolidated Interim Results for 6 months (Unaudited)

Profit & Loss Account

	Jun 30 1995	Jun 30 1996	
	£000s	£000s	
TURNOVER	1,783.0	2,487.0	+39.5
REP OPERATING PROF (LOSS)	155.0	458.0	+195.5
Interest income	–	4.0	n/a
Interest payable	(120.0)	(160.0)	+33.3
Excpl provisions	–	(40.0)	n/a
PROFIT (LOSS) BEFORE TAX	35.0	262.0	+648.6
PROFIT (LOSS) AFTER TAX	35.0	262.0	+648.6
Reported EPS(p)	0.10000	0.70000	+600.0

Balance Sheet

	Jun 30 1995	Jun 30 1996	
	£000s	£000s	
Intangible assets	10.0	13.0	+30.0
Tangible assets	9,285.0	7,816.0	-15.8
Financial assets	74.0	406.0	+448.6
FIXED ASSETS	9,369.0	8,235.0	-12.1
Debtors	805.0	986.0	+22.5
Cash & equivalents	374.0	614.0	+64.2
CURRENT ASSETS	1,179.0	1,600.0	+35.7
TOTAL ASSETS	10.548.0	9,835.0	-6.8
CREDS DUE WITHIN 1 YEAR	657.0	929.0	+41.4
NET CURR ASSETS (LIABS)	522.0	671.0	+28.5
ASSETS LESS CURR LIABS	9,891.0	8,906.0	-10.0
Other long term liabs	4,891.0	3,208.0	-34.4
Provisions	21.0	21.0	–
NET ASSETS (LIABS)	4,979.0	5,677.0	+14.0
SHARE CAPITAL	3,706.0	3,879.0	+4.7
RESERVES	1,273.0	1,798.0	+41.2
SHAREHOLDERS' FUNDS	4,979.0	5,677.0	+14.0
Net asset value (p)	–	23.60000	n/a
Gearing %	76.00000	46.00000	-39.5

Company Report	COMPANY RESEARCH	April 3, 1997

UNITED ENERGY PLC

CONSOLIDATED PROFIT AND LOSS ACCOUNT

	Dec 31 1991 £000	Dec 31 1992 £000	Dec 31 1993 £000	Dec 31 1994 £000	Dec 31 1995 £000
TURNOVER	377	2,794	3,003	2,520	4,125
Cost of sales	(345)	(1,900)	(1,986)	(1,909)	(2,913)
GROSS PROFIT	32	894	1,017	611	1,212
Administration exps	(303)	(831)	(791)	(786)	(715)
Other tdg inc (exp)	167	–	–	–	–
Misc other tdg inc	4	55	–	–	–
TRADING PROFIT (LOSS)	(100)	118	226	(175)	497
Interest income	46	19	3	3	20
Interest payable	(73)	(79)	(206)	(183)	(393)
Other expenses net	–	–	–	–	(13)
Exceptional charges	–	–	–	(24)	–
PROFIT (LOSS) BEF TAX	(127)	58	23	(379)	111
Tax	–	–	–	–	–
PROFIT (LOSS) AFT TAX	(127)	58	23	(379)	111
Ordinary dividends	–	–	–	–	–
RETD PROFITS (LOSSES)	(127)	58	23	(379)	111

NOTES TO CONSOLIDATED PROFIT AND LOSS ACCOUNT

	Dec 31 1991 £000	Dec 31 1992 £000	Dec 31 1993 £000	Dec 31 1994 £000	Dec 31 1995 £000
INTEREST PAYABLE					
Int within 5 yrs	(65)	(66)	(192)	(176)	(390)
Int after 5 yrs	(8)	(13)	(14)	(4)	–
Other charges	–	–	–	(3)	(3)
	(73)	(79)	(206)	(183)	(393)
EXCEPTIONAL CHARGES					
FA disposal gain	–	–	–	(24)	–
RETD PROFITS (LOSSES)					
Parent company	(93)	(622)	1,693	(61)	(121)
Subsidiaries	(34)	680	(1,670)	(318)	232
	(127)	58	23	(379)	111
PROFIT BEFORE TAX is after (charging) crediting					
Directors emoluments	(147)	(289)	(206)	(157)	(162)
Wages & salaries	(142)	(439)	(390)	(367)	(436)
Social security	(5)	(41)	(47)	(44)	(57)
Redundancy costs	–	(40)	(33)	–	–
Staff expenses	(147)	(520)	(470)	(411)	(493)
Auditors remuneration	(25)	(31)	(35)	(30)	(32)
Non-audit fees	(10)	(74)	(14)	(15)	(47)
Property provisions	–	–	–	–	(13)
Optg lease rentals	–	(36)	(39)	(38)	(53)
Depreciation	(5)	(32)	(41)	(39)	(24)
Amortn of intangibles	(230)	(1,036)	(1,066)	(1,035)	(1,527)
Av no of staff	5	14	12	12	13

GEOGRAPHICAL ANALYSIS – Turnover by source

	Dec 31 1992 £000	Dec 31 1993 £000	Dec 31 1994 £000	Dec 31 1995 £000
United Kingdom	410	675	452	57
USA	2,384	2,328	2,068	4,068
	2,794	3,003	2,520	4,125

GEOGRAPHICAL ANALYSIS – Profit before tax

	Dec 31 1992 £000	Dec 31 1993 £000	Dec 31 1994 £000	Dec 31 1995 £000
United Kingdom	(247)	130	(50)	(148)
USA	310	96	(125)	645
Net expenses	(5)	(203)	(204)	(386)
	58	23	(379)	111

UNITED ENERGY PLC

GEOGRAPHICAL ANALYSIS – Net Assets

	Dec 31 1992 £000	Dec 31 1993 £000	Dec 31 1994 £000	Dec 31 1995 £000
United Kingdom	634	928	573	860
USA	4,576	4,424	4,105	4,350
	5,210	5,352	4,678	5,210

CONSOLIDATED STATEMENT OF CASH FLOWS

	Dec 31 1991 £000	Dec 31 1992 £000	Dec 31 1993 £000	Dec 31 1994 £000	Dec 31 1995 £000
OPERATING ACTIVITIES	(321)	899	1,226	932	1,902
INVESTMENT RETURN AND SERVICING OF FINANCE					
Interest received	46	19	3	3	20
Interest paid	(73)	(79)	(206)	(183)	(393)
Other servicing infl	(5)	–	–	–	–
	(32)	(60)	(203)	(180)	(373)
TAXATION	–	–	–	–	–
INVESTING ACTIVITIES					
Subsidiaries acqd	–	(699)	–	–	–
Trade invs acquired	(41)	(1,724)	(798)	(978)	(5,249)
Tangibles acquired	(252)	(12)	(29)	(11)	(23)
Trade invs sold	105	123	34	1,354	340
Tangibles sold	–	1	4	217	–
	(188)	(2,311)	(789)	582	(4,932)
NET CASH FLOW BEFORE FINANCING	(541)	(1,472)	234	1,334	(3,403)
FINANCING					
Long term debt raised	182	2,436	698	369	4,305
Share capital issued	1	4	–	–	–
Long term debt repaid	–	(1,233)	(705)	(1,443)	(922)
	183	1,207	(7)	(1,074)	3,383
CASH INCR (DECR)	(358)	(265)	227	260	(20)

NOTES TO CONSOLIDATED STATEMENT OF CASH FLOWS

	Dec 31 1991 £000	Dec 31 1992 £000	Dec 31 1993 £000	Dec 31 1994 £000	Dec 31 1995 £000
OPERATING ACTIVITIES					
Trading profit (loss)	(100)	118	226	(175)	497
Depn & amortn incr	235	1,068	1,107	1,074	1,551
Provision increases	(252)	(60)	(50)	(18)	–
Other tdg adj incr	–	(219)	20	(18)	12
Decrease in debtors	91	(85)	106	203	(616)
Increase in creditors	(295)	77	(183)	(134)	458
	(321)	899	1,226	932	1,902
CASH INCR (DECR)					
Cash & near cash	(348)	(162)	434	(70)	(20)
Incr in overdrafts	(10)	(103)	(207)	330	–
	(358)	(265)	227	260	(20)

CONSOLIDATED BALANCE SHEETS

	Dec 31 1991 £000	Dec 31 1992 £000	Dec 31 1993 £000	Dec 31 1994 £000	Dec 31 1995 £000
FIXED ASSETS					
Intangible assets	–	274	240	13	13
Tangible assets	1,264	7,399	7,429	5,230	8,953
Financial assets	–	–	–	73	61
	1,264	7,673	7,669	5,316	9,027

UNITED ENERGY PLC

CURRENT ASSETS					
Trade debtors	–	697	515	408	1,027
Prepays/accrued inc	–	35	98	13	35
Other debtors	75	41	54	43	18
Cash & equivalents	359	197	631	561	541
	434	970	1,298	1,025	1,621
CREDS due within 1 yr					
Short term debt	23	136	343	–	–
Trade creditors	–	528	626	403	774
Accruals & defd inc	–	255	139	140	158
Tax & social security	–	–	3	5	6
Taxation	8	6	–	–	–
Other creditors	306	3	4	7	2
	337	928	1,115	555	940
NET CURRENT ASSETS	97	42	183	470	681
TOTAL ASSETS LESS CURRENT LIABILITIES	1,361	7,715	7,852	5,786	9,708
CREDS due after 1 yr					
Long term debt	179	2,221	2,256	1,087	4,477
Other L/T liabs	–	7	5	–	–
	179	2,228	2,261	1,087	4,477
PROVISIONS	49	277	239	21	21
NET ASSETS	1,133	5,210	5,352	4,678	5,210
Ordinary shares	1,248	3,366	3,366	3,366	3,705
Share premium	–	210	210	210	244
Capital reserves	–	928	928	928	928
Profit & loss account	(115)	706	848	174	333
SHAREHOLDERS' FUNDS	1,133	5,210	5,352	4,678	5,210

NOTES TO CONSOLIDATED BALANCE SHEETS

	Dec 31 1991 £000	Dec 31 1992 £000	Dec 31 1993 £000	Dec 31 1994 £000	Dec 31 1995 £000
TANGIBLE ASSETS					
Oth tangible FA-cost	–	–	10,099	8,818	14,116
Oth tang FA cost/valn	1,642	8,933	–	–	–
Oth tangible FA depn	(378)	(1,534)	(2,670)	(3,588)	(5,163)
Other tangible FA NBV	1,264	7,399	7,429	5,230	8,953
Tangible assets	1,264	7,399	7,429	5,230	8,953
FINANCIAL ASSETS					
Assoc company loans	–	–	–	61	61
Other trade invs	–	–	–	12	–
Trade investments	–	–	–	73	61
DEBT BY TYPE					
Bank loans	179	2,221	2,269	1,087	4,477
Bank lns & overdrafts	23	136	330	–	–
	202	2,357	2,599	1,087	4,477
DEBT BY MATURITY					
Short term loans	–	–	330	–	–
Current maturities	–	–	13	–	–
Debt due within 1 yr	23	136	–	–	–
Short term debt	23	136	343	–	–
Due within 1 to 2 yrs	–	13	13	1,087	–
Due within 2 to 5 yrs	–	2,097	2,146	–	4,477
Due after 5 years	–	111	97	–	–
Due after 1 year	179	–	–	–	–
	202	2,357	2,599	1,087	4,477

UNITED ENERGY PLC

DEBT BY SECURITY					
Secured	182	2,234	2,269	1,087	4,477
Unsecured	20	123	330	–	–
	202	2,357	2,599	1,087	4,477
Bank guarantees	–	–	–	1,090	4,480
Lease commitments	–	–	14	40	51

GENERAL NOTES TO ACCOUNTS

POST BALANCE SHEET EVENTS. In January 1996, the Group purchased a 30% shareholding in Agrigen with an option over a further 15% of the share capital for consideration of £150,000. In addition United Energy is making an interest bearing loan of £200,000 to Agrigen which is secured by a debenture over Agrigen's assets. In February 1996, the CBG litigation was settled out of court, with CNG paying AmBrit US$2.4m (£1.57m) to include purchase of AmBrit's Pennsylvania and West Viirginia properties. After the lawyers' contingency fees the amount due to the Group was US$2.05m (£1.34m). In accordance with the Group's accounting policy, the benefits arising from the settlement are to be recognised in the 1996 accounts as a deduction to the oil and gas interests cost pool on the Consolidated Balance Sheet. No benefits arising in respect of this settlement have been recognised in the 1995 accounts. In April 1996, AmBrit acquired a 74.8% working interest in the Ham Gossett Field for consideration of US$0.70m (£0.45m) in cash.

CHAIRMAN'S STATEMENT

The first quarter of 1996 has shown significant improvement over previous years with production well ahead and higher oil and gas prices comtributing to stronger cash flows and improved performance. Furthermore, our gearing is down to approximately 50% which, together with a stronger borrowing base as a result of reserve improvements, will enable acquisitions in excess of US$5m to be made this year without requiring further funds from shareholders. In addition, the Hare development well, combined with the Agrigen and the Ham Gossett acquisitions, indicate that 1996 could be an exciting year for United Energy.

ANNUAL GENERAL MEETING (year to 31-12-95)

Peel, Hunt and Co Ltd, 62 Threadneedle Street, London EC2R 8HP, on June 12 at 11.00am.

FINANCIAL CALENDAR

Interim Report 30th September 1996; Preliminary Figures 29th April 1996; Annual General Meeting 12th June 1996.

Copyright 1996
Telephone 0171-825-8888 – Fax 0171-608-3514
No responsibility accepted for error or omission
Extel is part of Financial Times Information   Licensed to Extel Financial Limited

Market Capitalisation. £7,370,460. This is a small company by any standards and consequently the risk factor is high if the economic climate deteriorated substantially and remained depressed for any significant length of time. The key to this risk lies in the chairman's statement which we shall discuss later.

TIP **As a general rule, low-priced shares denote a low market capitalisation and small trading volumes.** They almost always go hand in hand with a highly restricted 'market size'. For example, if the quote on the market is 24p to 28p, for up to 5,000 shares (the market size), beware of this restriction before you buy. The market maker will be only too happy to sell 50,000 shares to you when you are a buyer, but he may only be prepared to buy 5,000 shares back from you at the quoted price when you come to sell. If you are desperate to sell the remaining 45,000 shares, he may well drop the price for the balance to a figure where you may not even make a profit. Also, very often there may be two or three market makers only for low priced shares, so there is little or no room for your broker to 'shop around' to get rid of the extra shares at a reasonable price. It is doubtful whether execution-only brokers do much shopping around anyway.

PE Ratio. A PE ratio of 54.29 is very high in relation to the average for the sector. The interpretation of this is that the investor support is propping up the share price because there is a belief that the company will increase its earnings and that it will increase its dividends as a consequence, thus justifying the hopes of the investors. If that were to happen, and the share price were to remain where it is, then the PE Ratio would come down to a more realistic figure. Your reaction to this should be that the current picture looks fine for anyone who had bought in at around 12p, but at the present level it is expecting too much for the price to double again. Not what I would call a realistic proposition.

'By sticking to a low price range, you are asking for the share price to grow by a large amount per cent if your target profit is to be achieved.'

Activities. Development and production of proved and near proved oil and gas reserves in the USA and electricity generation from waste products in the UK. This means that the company is included in the category of fringe operator described above, with a bit of wild catting thrown in. Thus the earnings potential will be vulnerable to a drop in the price of oil or a rise in interest rates, although the gas market is likely to be more stable.

85

Table 4.1 Key Indicators: year-end 31 December

	1991	1992	1993	1994	1995
Earnings per share (EPS)	(1.02p)	0.19p	0.07p	(1.05p)	0.31p
Profit (loss) before Tax (£'000)	(127)	58	23	(379)	111
Trading Profit (loss) (£'000)	(100)	118	226	(175)	497
Shareholder's funds (£'000)	1,113	5,210	5,352	4,678	5,210
Return on capital employed (ROCE)	(8.98%)	2.26%	4.22%	(3.74%)	9.53%

The huge variation in the pre-tax profit record is typical of a company engaged in wild catting and the trading profit fluctuations bear this out. However, the results for the year ending 31 December 1995, together with the chairman's statement, will account for the rise in price in June 1996. In September 1996, the chairman made some more optimistic remarks about the company's progress and announced some successes in the drilling programme.

The share price *trend* will be unlikely to change direction until there is more news of progress (or lack of it) so any investment in this share at the current price would be extremely speculative.

The purpose of laying out this analysis is to show you that there is plenty of published information available to you and that you do not have to wade through mountains of paperwork or figures to be able to get quite enough of a feel for the company before you commit yourself.

I realise that this subsection is entitled *Sticking to a price range*, but you should still satisfy yourself that the share has more than a sporting chance of making the desired profit for you before you jump in. Furthermore, whilst I have selected an oil share for the purpose of an example and restricted my comments to the data shown in the key indices, I could have gone further into the analysis and looked at the debt progression for example, or cash flow, which is one of the most important aspects of any company whatever trade it is undertaking. However I have not done so, because this part of the book is devoted to short-term trading.

USING SOME OTHER METHOD OF SHARE SELECTION

The most obvious, and probably the one which most non-professional investors use is to subscribe to a tip sheet or follow the recommendations given by financial journalists. Reputations for success, or otherwise, vary enormously in this jungle and some might say that it is more of a lottery to follow such advice. Certainly a lot of the homework has been done for you and I have often found such tips have been very successful. But they have been successful for me only because although they were the catalyst which prompted me to look at a share. I subsequently did all my analysis and research into the background of the company, its markets, products, management and risk evaluation before I bought. **You should use them only as a starting point for further research**.

Don't forget that by the time you have read a newspaper or magazine, so have thousands of others. Their main use is to draw your attention to a share which you had not discovered or considered previously and alert you to what might turn out to be an interesting proposition.

Apart from the *Financial Times*, the most widely read journal is the *Investors Chronicle*, which adopts a fairly conservative approach to the way in which it lays out its information.

Figure 4.5 shows a typical page from the *Investors Chronicle*.

In addition to those described above, there are a number of newsletters issued by Fleet Street Publications. These include *The Penny Share Guide*, *The Fleet Street Letter*, *Stockmarket Confidential* and others which tend to adopt a more inquisitive approach. Figure 4.6 shows some typical pages from *Stockmarket Confidential*.

Their style is perhaps more entrepreneurial and this is no bad thing. But the same comment applies to these and any other sources of investment advice; use such tips as the beginning of your research, not as an end in itself. Of course it is very useful to have a potted version of relevant background data provided for you in a few words. Such information puts some flesh on the skeleton which emerges from the analysis of the Extel card data and, as such, improves your ability to

Fig 4.5 Typical page from the *Investors Chronicle*

COMPANY RESULTS

POWERGEN
Electricity generator

Good value

Ord price: 694p	Market value: £4.42bn	
Touch: 692-695p	12 month High:700p Low:462p	
Gross divd yield: 4.5%	PE ratio: 11	
Net asset value: 302p	Net debt: 34%	

Year to 31 Mar	Turn- over £bn	Pre-tax Profit £m	Stated Earnings per share (p)	Net Dividend per share (p)
1993	3.19	425	36.5	10.5
1994	2.93	476	44.0	12.7
1995	2.89	545	49.6	15.0
1996	2.93	687	71.4	21.0
1997	2.86	577	64.2	25.2
% Change −3		−16	−10	+20

Market makers: 19   Normal market size: 50,000
Last IC comment: 22 November 1996, page 65   xd: 2 June

Pre-exceptional profits edged up to £575m (£566m). This is a creditable achievement in a year when PowerGen leased two power stations to Eastern and its market share fell from 23 per cent to 21.6 per cent. At least this is a smaller drop in share than at National Power. Provisions of £67m against gas take-or-pay contracts in the now wholly owned Kinetica nearly wiped out all of the profit made on the sale of the Midlands Electricity stake. PowerGen believes the integration of Kinetica with the rest of the business will enable it to offer a fully bundled package of electricity, gas and energy management services.

PowerGen is behind National Power when it comes to generating profits overseas. International investments contributed the same as the previous year (£12m), although PowerGen is aiming for £100m by 2001. It's taking a 40 per cent share in a coal-fired power station in Indonesia and 30 per cent of another in Thailand. In all it has invested £700m in international projects.

Any windfall tax liability will be lower than that for National Power. Even a tax charge of about £300m would leave PowerGen with relatively low borrowings, giving it scope for acquisitions. The dividend is covered more than two and a half times, leaving room for growth. Despite the uncertainties of the windfall tax, the shares remain **attractive**.

CELLTECH
Drug researcher

Sell

Ord price: 343p	Market value: £260m	
Touch: 335-350p	12 month High: 672p Low: 333p	
Gross divd yield: nil	PE ratio: na	
Net asset value: 66p	Net cash: £41m	

Half-year to 31 Mar	Turn- over £m	Pre-tax Profit £m	Stated Earnings per share (p)	Net Dividend per share (p)
1996	0.10	−3.70	−5.20	nil
1997	2.00	−5.90	−7.90	nil
% Change +1900		−	−	−

Market makers: 9   Normal market size: 5,000
Last IC comment: 20 December 1996, page 53   xd:na

Celltech's results were overshadowed by last week's announcement that its septic-shock treatment, BAYX-1351, was ineffective. Royalties on sales of blood-clotting drug ReoPro by Centocor in the US rose to £2m from £0.9m in the second half of 1996. Income from milestone payments fell from £2.8m to £1m, all from Bayer, not expected to pay any more. Research and development spending rose 17 per cent to £10.1m. The main impact of the failure of BAYX-1351 will be to speed up development of treatments for leukaemia and Crohn's disease, but Celltech needs to find a partner for its psoriasis antibody earlier than it would have liked. Cash isn't a problem, but, with the company forecasting no profits until 2000, credibility is. **Sell**.

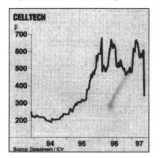

CELLTECH
Source: Datastream / ICV

ANGLIAN WATER
Water and sewerage services

Fairly priced

Ord price: 680p	Market value: £1.83bn	
Touch: 677-682p	12 month High: 700p Low: 523p	
Gross divd yield: 6.3%	PE ratio: 10	
Net asset value: 586p	Net debt: 59%	

Year to 31 Mar	Turn- over £m	Pre-tax Profit £m	Stated Earnings per share (p)	Net Dividend per share (p)
1993	583	185	56.4	21.1
1994	688	132	39.0	22.8
1995	720	216	66.4	26.0
1996	776	239	78.1	30.0
1997	837	208	68.6	34.5
% Change +8		−13	−12	+15

Market makers: 16   Normal market size: 25,000
Last IC comment: 8 November 1996, page 58   xd: 30 Aug

Profits before a £41m exceptional charge were at the top of analysts' forecasts at £257m. Cost savings helped: Anglian says that by next March the measures it has taken will save £50m a year. Although reservoirs are only 70 per cent full, Anglian is confident it won't have to inflict any restrictions on its customers. Its leakage rate has been reduced from 13 per cent to 11.8 per cent – one of the lowest in the industry.

Anglian is paying £19.5m for the second-smallest water company in Britain, Hartlepool Water, which covers just 90 square kilometres of Teesside. It wants to use Hartlepool as a base to supply industrial customers in the adjacent area. This will bring it into competition with the French-owned Northumbrian Water. Anglian Water International continues to perform disappointingly. It lost £6.1m (£5.7m) and provisions of £19m have been made for restructuring and asset write-downs.

Anglian's contribution to the windfall tax debate is that the proceeds raised from it should be spent in its local area. Water companies look likely to be hit the hardest, and Anglian's borrowings are already pretty high, especially as capital spending – £354m last year – remains heavy. Even on best-case scenarios Anglian may have to pay £150m-£200m tax. Until these uncertainties are cleared up the shares are **about right**.

WARNING

■ **MARKETABILITY** Our UK company results tables contain the following information to help assess how easy it will be to buy or sell shares.

Touch This is the narrowest spread available in the market between a buy and sell price. The larger the difference between the two, the more difficult it will be to deal.

Normal Market Size Each share has a normal market size between 500 and 200,000, based on the average size of deals made over the past 12 months. Market makers are only obliged to stick

to their spread if the bargain is within the normal size. The larger it is, the easier it is to buy and sell; the smaller it is, the more difficult.

Number of Market Makers The largest companies tend to have the most market makers dealing in their shares, and their shares are the easiest to trade. If a company has fewer than three market makers, dealing is likely to be difficult.

SEATS/Bulletin Board Shares traded on these two systems are extremely difficult to deal in. The bulletin board is a matched bargain system. That means

you cannot buy or sell shares unless another party is prepared to trade in the opposite direction. SEATS combines the bulletin board with one market maker.

■ **COMPANY PROFITS AND EARNINGS** Companies have adopted a new accounting standard that may substantially affect their profits and earnings per share, more often down than up. As they have all adopted it, we will no longer mark our company results tables to show those affected.

Fig 4.6 Typical example of pages from *Stockmarket Confidential*

Profits from 'The Big Match'

Insiders – Buying at Caspian Group ☆☆☆

After analysing the two-dozen companies in which directors have bought their own shares since our last issue, I am focusing on

Caspian Group – once known as Storm Group – which has become a major beneficiary from the City's love affair with football. I spotted that Chris Akers, Caspian's chairman, had bought 100,000 shares in the company at 43.5p apiece for £43,500 to take his holding to 2,950 shares.

Caspian is a former media group – now listed in the *Financial Times* under 'Leisure' – which made a big acquisition in 1996. This was the City's first major expansion into the world of football, which is now awash with cash as clubs crowd on to the stock market while the going is good. And the City is particularly keen on the Premier League clubs. Caspian had impeccably blue-blooded City backers. Run by former merchant banker Chris Akers, the company recently bought Leeds United in a hotly contested deal worth about £30m – thereby winning the first ever City-backed takeover battle for a football club. Experts described the deal as a steal. There is almost £8m available for new players.

THE KEY FACTS – CASPIAN GROUP	
Financial Times listing:	Leisure & Hotels
Sharecall Directory code:	05280
Share price:	36p (do not pay more than 38p)
Trading range:	10.5p to 47.5p
Market capitalisation:	£102.6m
Head office:	106 Gloucester Place, London W1H 3DR (tel: 0171-935 1596)

Paving the way for the deal

Richard Thompson, the former chairman, paved the way for the deal by more than halving his holding in Caspian – selling 1.5m of his shares to Chris Akers, a former Swiss Bank Director who masterminded the reverse takeover of Freepages, and a further 6.5m to private investors all at 12p per share – but still has a 7% stake and a seat on the board.

The battle for Leeds United reflects the rising City interest in football. Caspian was up against a rival group, Conrad, which pitched in a significantly higher bid. However, Leeds United went to Caspian because it offered a better future and the club was also impressed by Caspian's City connections.

Tipping the balance in Caspian's favour with their combined 66% shareholding was Leeds chairman Bill Fotherby and his predecessor Leslie Silver. They preferred Caspian's 80p a share to Conrad's £1 and opted for Caspian's £10m to £12m investment compared with Conrad's £15m to £17m. 13.2m shares, or 66% of Leeds issued capital, was bought from the two at 82.5p per share.

Blue chip backers

Caspian is owned by blue chip investors including Schroders, Mercury Asset Management, London and Manchester and Guardian Royal Exchange. Virtually all the money Caspian is investing in the club is being spent on the team and none of it is being used to reduce Leeds United's £10m of debt. Caspian aims to become the UK's largest sports and leisure group by building up a portfolio of interests in football, rugby and other sports.

Caspian intends to establish an ice hockey and a basketball franchise in Leeds. Chris Akers hopes the new teams will play at the sports, entertainment and retail complex which Caspian is intending to build alongside Elland Road, Leeds United's 40,000-seater stadium. The funds were raised by a £30m placing and open offer at 18.5p per share and a £2m offer for subscription at the same price. Additionally Caspian subscribed £12m for 12m new Leeds United shares to take its holding to 93.6%. Another £5.6m is to be made available if required.

The latest trading picture

Given the massive change in the nature of Caspian's business, historic figures provide only a little background of useful information. Caspian reported a lower pre-tax loss of £1.12m in 1995 against a £1.85m loss last time after a £572,000 exceptional charge. Turnover was £1.88m against £2.4m. In the last half year to 30 June 1996 Caspian made a pre-tax loss of £80,000 against £541,000 on turnover of £1.16m against £768,000 last time. During the first half of the latest year, FilmFair Animation continued work on the fifth series of Astrofarm for the ITV Network. The group's existing sports interests, comprising Multi Media Television Productions, JHA and Racing World all performed satisfactorily during the first half. Multi Media Television Productions produced a further series of *Sport in Question* for Carlton TV and continued as producer of the Racing Channel for BSkyB. The interim results for the latest six months don't include any contribution from Leeds United or the impact of the funds raised under the placing and open offer. The big change resulting from the acquisition has meant a change of year-end from 31 December to 30 June – so the next results to be reported will be the group's interim results for the six months to end-December 1996.

High calibre new management

Robin Launders has been appointed chief executive of Leeds United and George Graham has been appointed manager – both high-calibre appointments.

After five successful years as finance director at Manchester United, Launders is ideally suited to bring some shine to the Caspian share price. the shares have doubled since it clinched the Leeds United deal and investors hope it can repeat the Red Devils

astonishing financial success. Chinese and Italian food outlets are sprouting up in the ground and there is a 8,400 sq ft merchandise shop which has cost nearly £1m, with further plans for outlets in the city centre and elsewhere in Yorkshire.

Trading levels well up

Current trading levels at Leeds United are well up on the comparable figures for last year. Football turnover is enhanced by new kit and club sponsorship deals, increased TV income via the Premier League and from sales through the new retail outlets.

Caspian has been talking to the Leeds Rugby League club about a takeover and to Yorkshire Cricket club about finding a solution to the latter's need for new capital. Even if Leeds United does not regain dominance and Caspian's plans are medium rather than long term, the team needs only to survive in the world's wealthiest league for Caspian to benefit from the cash pouring into football.

Caspian selling under-performing operations

Caspian has been shedding under-performing operations – it has sold off its catalogue of children's television programmes and rights to characters such as the Wombles for £10.5m to Cinar Films. This resulted from the sale of FilmFair, the subsidiary which owns the majority of Caspian's children's characters. FilmFair made a loss of £678,659 for the year to end-December 1995. Without making acquisitions in the same area – which it failed to find – Caspian's existing catalogue did not represent a sufficiently commercial proposition. Bearing in mind that Caspian bought the catalogue in 1991 for £1.75m, the sale to Cinar for £10.5m was a useful bonus.

SMC verdict

Caspian offers an outstanding opportunity to take a stake in the stock market's love affair with sport.

form a judgement. It all helps to diminish the areas of the unknown and thereby reduce the risk of overlooking something vital which, had you but only known at the time, would have prevented you from regretting your investment at a later date.

Financial journalists and analysts are as prone to individual prejudices and preferences as anyone else. Like racing tipsters, they can't pick winners every day of the week. But they do an essential job because their criticism is read by the management of the companies which they put under the spotlight just as avidly as it is by investors looking for a chance to make money. You will find by experience which ones are consistently better at producing relevant comment on the shares in the sector of your choice and it will pay you to include their pronouncements in your list of areas for research. The *Investors Chronicle* will send you detailed reports of individual companies, for a fee, which can be most useful.

SUMMARY

In this chapter we have described ways in which you can find types of shares for investment opportunities. We have discussed:

- specialising in a sector with particular reference to areas of trade or interest in which the investor has acquired experience and demonstrating the kind of knowledge which will be required, using the oil sector as an example;
- sticking to a price range and explaining why low priced shares have inherent dangers when it comes to selling;
- following recommendations from tip sheets and financial journalists.

TECHNICAL ANALYSIS AND FUNDAMENTAL ANALYSIS

In this chapter we examine the uses and applications of the following analytical tools:

- technical analysis
- fundamental analysis
- the three basic types of charts
- Fibonacci fan lines.

TECHNICAL ANALYSIS

Technical analysis can be described as the study of market action, mainly through the use of charts, for the purpose of forecasting future price trends. It can be applied to stock markets, unit trusts, shares, commodities, currencies etc.

Technical analysis is based on three premises:

1. Market action discounts everything, i.e., all known information is reflected in the prices.
2. Prices move in trends, and trends persist. A trend in motion will continue until it is reversed.
3. History repeats itself in the form of easily recognisable market trading patterns, i.e., the future is just a repetition of the past.

At first sight, the statements made above may look a little facile, but in fact these premises are used by a very large number of analysts and fund managers as well as by individual traders who make a living on their own account in such volatile markets as financial futures, spread betting and option trading. There are obviously a number of fallacies which are contained in these premises and I should like to discuss a few of them at this point before continuing, but do not dismiss these statements made above, because in fact they are valuable if you know how to apply them and you have to remember that you use them within a clearly defined time scale.

Let us take the first point: 'Market action discounts everything'. Well, that is not true, for the simple reason that unexpected things happen, chairmen die, rogue traders such as Leeson at Barings create havoc without anybody knowing about them beforehand, and therefore it cannot be said of the market that all the information is reflected in the prices. The comment actually is meant to demonstrate that the prices of shares are based upon such information as is known through the media, through analytical dissection of the accounts and from all the latest information released by those companies whose shares are listed on the market. To that extent, the statement that the market reaction discounts everything that is known, is true.

Share prices are based upon current and future earnings and the earnings are declared in audited accounts so that there is an independent corroboration of the management's declared results. Consequently, forecasts of the future direction which the earnings are likely to take are based on fact, and market opinion of such assessments assume that all relevant facts are known, so to that extent the statement is true. Obviously, there will occur events which are beyond any form of prediction, and these can have a dramatic effect on the market price.

> '... it cannot be said of the market that all the information is reflected in the prices.'

Statement number 2 says that 'prices move in trends, and trends persist'. This is very true because if you look at the share price over a very short period such as a matter of hours, or indeed over a long period such as a matter of years, then trends can be established quite easily, and if you trade within those periods you will find that technical analysis can be of considerable help to you. The statement that a trend in motion will continue until it is reversed is a little bit facile, but what it is trying to say is that a trend is something which has a momentum of its own and you should follow it and be advised to take it into your consideration because no individual action will change it. The trend will change of its own accord.

The third statement about history repeating itself is equally true. This will be demonstrated when we come to consider spread betting later in this chapter, and you will see that this item forms the basis of the overall strategy.

FUNDAMENTAL ANALYSIS

Fundamental analysis is the study of historical data such as dividends, earnings, profit and loss accounts, balance sheets, etc., to try to arrive at a fair value for an individual share, or for the market as a whole. If the current market price is lower than the estimate of its current value, then analysts would issue an advice to buy. If their analysis indicated the opposite, they would advise selling.

It is possible that such historic evaluation of an individual share might demonstrate that the current price is well below its true value, but that until a sufficient number of ordinary and institutional investors discover this anomaly and start to buy the share, the price may remain undervalued for a very long time. I think that the possibility is remote because the Press and financial intermediaries are constantly on the alert for undervalued shares, and if there is sufficient reason for them to recommend a share which looks cheap, then they will do so with as much energy as possible.

THE DIFFERENCE BETWEEN TECHNICAL ANALYSIS AND FUNDAMENTAL ANALYSIS

Technical analysis is the study of price action *to the exclusion of all other factors*. By using certain mathematical formulae, technical analysts calculate whether an individual share or market is trading on an historically cheap or expensive basis. They use charts to plot the movement of prices to see whether a particular share is being bought or sold and consequently they can advise when is the right time to buy or sell. Timing is of the essence, and in these days of volatile markets, getting the timing right is of paramount importance, particularly if you are going to trade short-term, and even more so if you are going to play with spread betting.

Both forms of analyses are important because the ability to identify overvalued or undervalued assets using fundamental analysis methods is essential and if you combine it with the ability to get the timing right by using technical analysis, you have a very powerful combination tool in your bag.

CHARTS

These are the most important tools in the technical analyst's trade, and there are three types which are most commonly used.

The three basic types of chart are:

- Bar charts
- Line charts
- Point and figure charts

There are several others but we shall confine our examination to these three.

Bar Charts

A bar chart can be constructed to show the daily, weekly monthly or yearly price range which is represented by a vertical bar for each period. A horizontal tick is placed to the right of the bar to indicate the level at which the price closed. On some charts a horizontal tick is also placed to the left of the bar to indicate the opening price. They will usually show the trading volume at the base of the bar. As a general rule, if prices close near to the top of their range on the day, the indication is that the pressure is on the buying side of the market and further price rises are likely to follow on subsequent trading days. If the prices close near to the bottom of their trading range then the reverse is true.

An example of a screen showing a bar chart appears in Figure 5.1 and it records the daily opening and closing prices for British Airports Authority as well as the volumes of shares traded for the two-year period beginning June 1995 and ending May 1997. A line chart is also shown covering the same period.

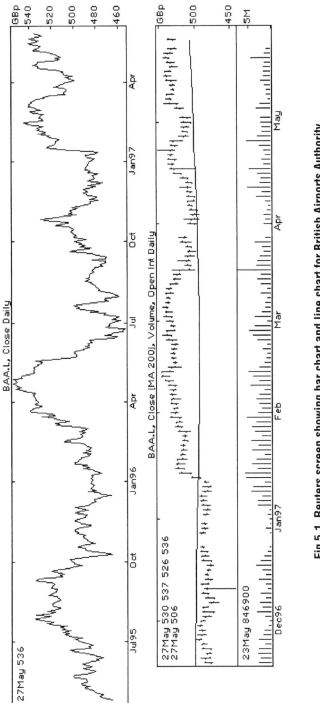

Fig 5.1 Reuters screen showing bar chart and line chart for British Airports Authority
(Source: Reuters)

You will realise from this that a share price can and often does establish a trading range during a day as well as over longer periods. To be successful at making money in such markets, you will have to have access to real-time prices and be glued to the screen for the duration of your exposure to the risk while you remain invested in the share or future or option.

There is a considerable amount of learning required if you are going to become adept at interpreting these charts and you will require to undertake further reading on the subject.

However, for our purposes, they are useful because they demonstrate one particular point which is fundamental to any trader. It is frequently the case that during the day, a share price will move up or down by quite large amounts after the market has opened and yet it ends the day not much above or below its opening price.

Figure 5.2 shows the bar chart and Figure 5.3 shows the line chart for British Airports Authority recording the daily price movements as well as the opening and closing figures from 19 November 1996 to 27 May 1997, and if you look at the bars between 8 April and 22 April, you will see a good example of the price volatility during one day on several occasions.

By watching and recording these closing prices, you are establishing the trend over a short term. They say that the trend is your friend, and so it is. The reason is that the market is trying to tell you something. If there appears to be sustained demand for a share during the day (or the opposite) and the share price ends up not too far away from its opening price, then the market is telling you that the fair price *in the market* is somewhere near its closing price. This price may not bear much relation to a fair value established through fundamental analysis; it is demonstrating market forces at work. Thus, if the trend over a period is depressed, then the share is gradually losing favour and you would be well-advised to avoid buying it, or to sell it if you hold it already.

Second, if you want to trade a share, or future, or option for very small percentage profits over a few hours at a time, it is essential to know the amount of movement, or trading range, during the day. Obviously if the profit potential is small for such short-term trades,

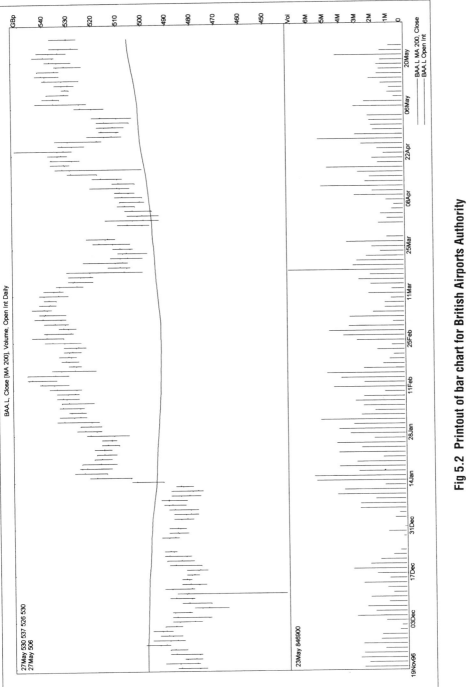

Fig 5.2 Printout of bar chart for British Airports Authority

(Source: Reuters)

Fig 5.3 Printout of line chart for British Airports Authority

(Source: Reuters)

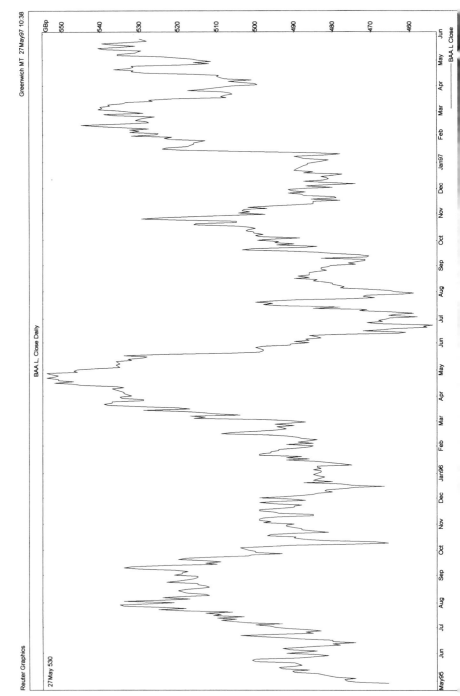

then you will have to risk quite large sums of capital to make the exercise worth while.

Line Charts

Line charts are the most familiar type in use and they simply show the closing prices which are connected by a solid line.

Point and Figure Charts

Point and figure charts are entirely different from bar or line charts in as much as they only record price action and they do not have a fixed time scale.

They are plotted on squared graph paper and appear as vertical columns of Os and Xs, where each O or X represents a certain value, which is normally around 1 per cent of the current market price or index level.

Rising prices are represented by Xs, falling prices by Os. A reversal factor is used to decide when prices should be plotted in the opposite direction, and as a rule of thumb guide, a reversal factor of 3 normally produces the best results.

> '... the establishment of trend lines and the ability to calculate future support and resistance levels is of paramount importance'

The importance of point and figure charts is that they can provide extremely accurate price target forecasts, buy and sell signals, highlight support and resistance levels and reveal consolidation areas and trading ranges with much more clarity than can be seen on bar and line charts.

As I said earlier in this book, the establishment of trend lines and the ability to calculate future support and resistance price levels is of paramount importance, particularly for the short-term trader. So at the risk of repeating myself, I shall redefine them.

An uptrend is a series of higher highs and higher lows. A downtrend is a series of lower highs and lower lows. A sideways trend is often called a 'consolidation', and the highs and lows will be horizontal. Very often, when a consolidation occurs, the highs get lower and the lows get higher, so that the picture resembles a funnel on its side. When this happens, it is the precursor of a change in direction in the trend and you should watch the chart closely to see which way the new trend establishes itself before you commit yourself. It is most unwise to try to trade a share in such a configuration, however short the period being contemplated.

Trend Fan-line Formations

In an uptrend, a straight line is drawn from the low point on the chart connecting with the first major correction (the first substantial high), and extended. When this first trend line is penetrated in a downward direction, the second line is drawn from the same low point connecting with the second reaction low. This process is repeated until there are four trend lines drawn one below the other in a fan formation.

A warning that the uptrend is under threat is given when the closing price falls below the first trend line. A break through downwards of the second trend line is the signal to sell. A break of the third line usually confirms a trend reversal, but quite often a bounce will occur, giving you a chance to sell before the price breaks through the fourth trend line in the fan formation. The same method can be applied to a downtrend by drawing the fan trend lines from the high point on the chart connecting the rally highs.

Support and Resistance

Resistance is a price level or zone above the market where selling pressure can be expected to check or even reverse a price advance. A previous peak will often represent a resistance level, but prices will also meet resistance following advances measured in percentage terms. These levels, which might be called natural levels, can occur at 12.5 per cent, 16.6 per cent, 25 per cent, 33.3 per cent, 50 per cent, 66.6 per cent, 75 per cent and 100 per cent, with 25 per cent increases thereafter.

Support is a price level or zone below the current market price where increased buying can be expected to check any price fall. A previous low will often represent a support level, but prices will also meet support following declines measured in percentage terms as shown above for resistance.

Once a support or resistance level has been penetrated decisively, it will reverse its role. In an uptrend, for example, once a resistance level has been broken by a reasonable margin, it will then act as a support level on a subsequent decline. In a downtrend the reverse will apply.

It will be found in most cases that resistance is always stronger than support. This is due to the fact that emotions associated with getting out of the market are much greater than those associated with getting in, i.e. the fear of loss is much greater than the desire for gain.

A good example of this principle can be seen by looking at the share price history of Boots over the 12-month period June 1996 to June 1997. In Figure 5.4 you can see the line chart covering this period.

Figure 5.5 shows the same chart with the line AB superimposed. If you had been looking at this chart in February 1997, and you had to forecast the future direction of the share price, you would have been able to draw the following conclusions:

- The highs which occurred between August/September and during October reached a resistance level of about 640p which was penetrated weakly in January/February 1997.
- At that time, it would have been difficult to forecast, except to say that if the line were to move more positively in an upward direction above the line AB, then it would signal a strong buy. Thus, you would have wanted to watch the daily progress very closely and be prepared to act quickly if the movement gave a strong signal.
- In February/March 1997, the price moved decisively upwards to around 700p, so that a projection of the line AB into the future would have given you a support level if the share price started to fall back. The line AB which had been a resistance level up to that time has now become a support level.

Figure 5.6 shows the same chart with the addition of the line CD which had been a resistance level at about 700p from February/March 1997 until it was decisively penetrated in an upward direction in

Fig 5.4 Printout of line chart for Boots
(Source: Topic)

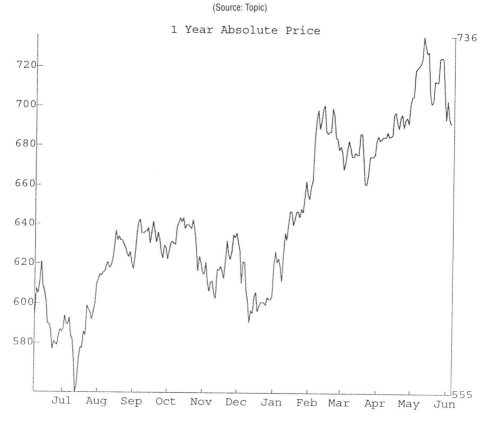

April/May 1997, whereupon it became a support level. This is demonstrated by the way the share price dropped towards it in May from a high of 736p and then rebounded back to a level of about 722p.

In June 1997, the price penetrated the line CD downwards positively before rebounding back to the line CD which it failed to penetrate strongly and has continued to drop below the line CD since then. Thus the line CD has now reverted to being a resistance level once again. If you had to make a forecast for the future at this time, you would be safe with the following observations:

- A weak resistance level appears to be at around the 685p mark. You can see this if you extend a line from the high of 685p which occurred in March/April through the small high at the same price

Fig 5.5 Printout of line chart for Boots with resistance/support level at 640p

(Source: Topic)

which occurred about four weeks later.

- If the share price penetrates this weak resistance level downwards positively, then the next resistance level will be 640p.
- If the share price continues to drop below the 640p level, the next resistance level will occur at 620p and after that at 555p.

The difference in money terms between support and resistance levels gives the short term trader a very good *practical* idea of how much potential profit or loss is achievable by buying and selling within the price movements, and depending upon the amount of potential profit these levels indicate, the trader can calculate whether there is enough potential upside to make such an investment a worthwhile proposition.

Fig 5.6 Printout of line chart for Boots with resistance/support level at 700p
(Source: Topic)

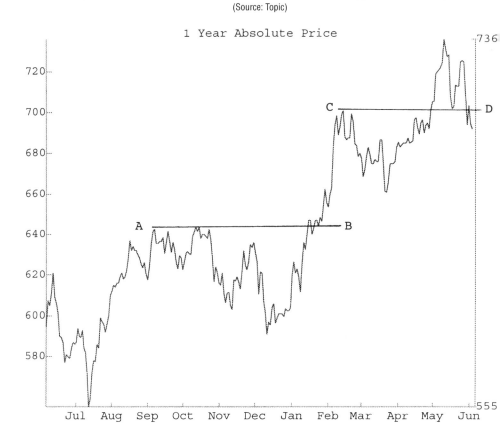

The time it will take for such an investment to bear fruit will be further refined by including short-term indicators as well in your calculations, and this subject is dealt with next.

SHORT-TERM INDICATORS

Overbought/oversold

Markets are said to be overbought or oversold when aggressive buying or selling has moved current prices too far too fast in either direction. The same applies to individual shares. This action is likely to be followed by a correction or a consolidation in prices before the original trend can be resumed.

Oscillators, or short-term indicators (STIs) are really only useful for looking back over a relatively short period of time, and for short-term trading.

Most traders envisage 'STIs' as an acceleration or deceleration indicator because the *speed* of the rise or fall plays a very significant part in decision-making for short-term trades.

Assume you are driving a car and imagine taking your foot off the accelerator pedal. You may not notice any dramatic change in your speed, or forward momentum, but you begin to feel a reversal from acceleration forward to deceleration, or a gradual slowing down of momentum.

Relative Strength Indicator (RSI)

This indicator is probably the most important signal showing whether a market or individual share is overbought or oversold. It can be applied to shares as well as futures or options. To give an example, we shall use the FTSE 100 index.

Relative strength (RS) is calculated as follows:

$$RS = \frac{\text{Average of } n \text{ day's 'up' closes}}{\text{Average of } n \text{ day's 'down' closes}}$$

(where n = the number of days).

You can use any time period to establish the moving average and for the purpose of this example, we shall take 14 trading days.

Thus n = 14

To find the average 'up' value for 14 days, you add together the number of points on a daily basis between the opening figure and the closing figure of the FTSE 100 *where the closing figure was higher than the opening figure*. Divide this sum by 14 to get the average 'up' close.

To find the average 'down' value you add together the number of points on a daily basis between the opening figure and closing figure of the FTSE 100 *where the closing figure was lower than the opening figure*. Divide this sum by 14 to get the average 'down' close.

RS is then determined by dividing the **up** average by the **down** average.

The relative strength indicator (RSI) is calculated by using the following formula:

$$RSI = 100 - \frac{[100]}{RS}$$

There are PC software programs available which will do these calculations for you very quickly so that you can see the overbought/oversold position at a glance without having to do all the tedious calculations yourself.

Fibonacci fan lines

Leonardo Fibonacci was a 13-century mathematician who devised a solution to the mathematical problem involving the reproduction of rabbits! The number sequence he produced is written as 1,1,2,3,5,8,13,21,34,55,89,144 and so on to infinity.

The sequence has a number of interesting properties, not the least of which is an almost constant relationship between the numbers, i.e., the sum of any two consecutive numbers equals the next higher number. For example, 3+5=8, 5+8=13 and so on.

The ratio of any number to its next higher number approaches **0.618** after the first four numbers. For instance, 1 to1 is 1.00; 1 to 2 is 0.5; 2 to 3 is 0.67; 5 to 8 is 0.625; 8 to 13 is 0.615; 13 to 21 is 0.619 etc.

The ratio of any number to its next lower number is approximately 1.618, or the inverse of 0.618. For example, 13 to 8 is 1.625; 21 to 13 is 1.615; 34 to 21 is 1.619. The higher the numbers become, the closer the values become to 0.618 and 1.618.

In fact, although Fibonacci published his findings, the ratio of 1.618 and 0.618 was known to the ancient Greek and Egyptian mathematicians and was called the Golden Ratio. The Greeks used it in constructing the Parthenon and the Egyptians employed it in building the Pyramids. The ratio was known to Pythagoras, Plato and Leonardo da Vinci.

The practical application of Fibonacci ratios

The Fibonacci ratios help to determine price objectives as well as impulse and corrective waves. One way to determine price objectives is by the use of percentage retracements. The most commonly used numbers in retracement analysis are 61.8 per cent; 50 per cent and 38 per cent.

It should be noted that markets usually retrace previous moves by certain predictable percentages, the best known being 33 per cent; 50 per cent and 62 per cent. The Fibonacci sequence refines these numbers a bit further. In a strong trend, the minimum retracement is usually around 38 per cent and in a weak market the maximum percentage retracement is usually around 62.

It is possible to use Fibonacci numbers in setting time targets by counting forward from significant tops and bottoms. On a daily chart, the analyst counts forward the number of trading days from an important turning point with the expectation that future tops or bottoms will occur on Fibonacci days, i.e. the 13th; 21st; 34th; 55th or 89th trading day in the future. The same technique can be used on weekly, monthly or even yearly charts.

All traders on the dealing floors use Fibonacci for anticipating the amount by which the commodity or index they are trading will rise or fall in the period ahead, as well as the resistance and support levels in that particular market. It is used for hourly, daily, weekly, monthly or yearly forecasting.

Let us take an example.

On 24 April 1997, the FTSE 100 index produced the following marks:

Low for the day	4394
High for the day	4422
Close at 17.30	4415

The reason for waiting until 17.30, one hour after the London market has shut is because Wall Street is still open and it is desirable to get the latest data possible for accuracy of forecasting.

The FTSE had been on an upward trend on the 23 April.

Table 5.1 shows how Fibonacci ratios were calculated and used to set support and resistance levels for trading on the 25 April.

Table 5.1: Fibonacci ratios for setting support and resistance levels

			4415			
		4394		4422		
	4382	4399	4410	4427	4438	
	2nd support	1st support	pivot	1st resistance	2nd resistance	
0%		4422		4399		0.00
23.6%		4415		4401		6.61
38.2%		4411		4405		10.70
50%		4408		4408		14.0
61.8%		4405		4411		17.3
76.4%		4401		4415		21.39
100%		4394		4422		28.0
			Key levels of support and resistance			

If the FTSE moves upwards through the first resistance to somewhere near the second resistance, then the first resistance becomes a support level. Likewise if the FTSE falls to somewhere near the second support, then the first support becomes a resistance level.

The system works on the principle of moving averages which is the basis of W.D. Gann or the Elliot Wave theory. To understand these analytical methods of forecasting, further reading is recommended because the subjects are too complex to include here.

If all the rather technical explanation given so far has left you feeling slightly bemused, let me describe the basic system in layman's language. The first most important point is to understand what an **average** is. It is the mid-point between a high and a low. Consider the measurement of the tides. The sea water ebbs and flows daily, but the volume of water varies daily. At the time of new and full moons, the high tides are higher and the low tides are lower. These are called the 'spring tides'. In between these spring tides, the high tides are less high and the low tides less low. These are called the 'neap tides'.

If the volume of water flowing in and out increases *by the same amount* each day between the neaps and the springs, and decreases by the same amount each day between the springs and the springs, the *average* point between high and low water will remain in exactly the same position. Thus if you were to plot the *average* point on a chart for each day it would project in a straight line. So would the *trend line* because although the 'highs' would fluctuate producing a formation of peaks and troughs, the 'lows' would give the same picture upside down because the measurement between each high and each low *from the mid-point* would be equal for each day. The highs would gradually be getting higher but the lows would gradually be getting lower *by the same amount*.

Likewise if you plotted the 30-day, 90-day or 200-day *moving average*, it would also be a straight line.

But if you put the **time** on the chart as a subdivision of each day and connected the highs to the lows with a line, you would get a picture which resembles somewhat those print-outs which you sometimes see on the television of a lie detector in action. The recording arm moves up and down rapidly when certain questions are asked of the victim, and if the movement becomes exaggerated for a short period, it is supposed to indicate that the answer which has been given is false. This is called 'oscillation'.

The second important point is to learn the lesson which these 'pictures' show. *In every case the line on the chart returns from the previous high and cuts through the average on its way to the next low, in the example of the tides.*

Tides are predictable and follow a strict pattern throughout the year, so the moving average will follow a straight line as I have described. However, suppose that there was an underwater earthquake somewhere out in the ocean which produced a tidal wave out of the blue. Suddenly the 'high' mark would be very much higher than anything recorded on the chart so far. Further suppose that the phenomenon interfered with the ebb tide for a period so that the highs and lows became erratic and followed a different pattern than before. During that period, the average point would be different from the previous ones and the line connecting them would not be straight any more. The trend line would change also. *But the lines connecting the highs and lows would still oscillate above and below the changing average line.*

So the lesson to be learned is that when you record the movement of something which is dynamic and which does not progress in a straight line over a period of time, however long or brief the period may be, the movement will be one of constant departure from and returning towards the average.

> **The secret is to be able to predict the direction of the movement and measure its extent either away from or towards the moving average, as well as the speed of advance and retraction.**

Figure 5.7, which is taken from the 30 May issue of the *Investors Chronicle* shows a very good example of the chart of the FTSE 100 together with the 20-day, 50-day and 200-day moving averages.

The simplest way of using Fibonacci for short-term traders is to buy a software program, and install it on your PC where it will carry out all the calculations for you in seconds, so that you can be advised of the support and resistance levels instantly on your screen. For this sort of trading you will need access to real-time data feed and you will have to shop around to find a supplier who will give you access to the database at a price within your budget.

> '… when you record the movement of something which is dynamic and which does not progress in a straight line over a period of time … the movement will be one of constant departure from and returning towards the average.'

In the next chapter devoted to spread betting, I demonstrate a rather more simplified way of using the Fibonacci principles which can be very effective, so do not be put off by the deeper and more technical explanation given above.

Fig 5.7 Investors Chronicle commentary with chart of the FTSE 100 with 20-day, 50-day and 200-day moving averages

(Sources: Datastream/CV and *Investors Chronicle*)

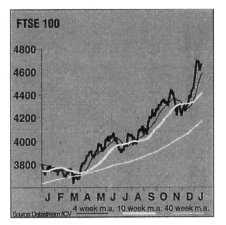

WHERE is the uptrend after the volatility of recent days? **The FTSE** 100 index (4607) is close to testing its four-week moving average as I write. If that is broken then the 10-week is at 4450, where a test would place the index in the centre of the parallels drawn upwards from last winter. That would be reassuring for the bulls as a setback of 250 points would leave the index still well placed for further upward progress.

But is there hope here for the bears? The index was so overbought and exposed to a change of investment sentiment, when it was up on a spike close to 4700, that a sell-off was inevitable. Nothing surprising about that. Equity prices invariably fall back into a set of parallels when well through the top line. That is one of the key reasons why they are such a useful tool in assessing the likely direction of a trend.

There is also the 40-week moving average to give encouragement to investors currently holding a bearish view of prospects for the market. At some point in time, the index will meet the long-term moving average again. That average will be placed close to 4200

by our publication date and it does not need emphasising too much that a fall to that level would destroy a lot of capital.

With so much that is uncertain about, I must again urge readers to move out of their calls if my stop limit seems likely to come under pressure. We must remember that a level of 4700 would have seemed a very bullish forecast as recently as the middle of April.

While the bulls dream of the index climbing through 5000, let's make sure that we don't slide with them if their optimism proves to be unfounded.

SUMMARY

In this chapter we have examined the following essential tools for short-term trading analysis to enable you to set targets which are achievable:

- technical analysis, which studies the actions of markets, indices or individual shares and enables you to establish trends and measure them accurately;
- fundamental analysis, which involves the study of audited results from the *Annual Report & Accounts* to enable you to establish fair value;
- the three basic types of chart, the different signals which they give out and the usefulness of each one;
- trend fan-line formations and their value in showing support and resistance levels for control of the management of your individual investments;
- Fibonacci ratios and the way they are calculated and applied. We have demonstrated particularly their value when trading in the very short-term.

SPREAD
BETTING

INTRODUCTION

Spread betting, as the name says, is a form of gambling no different essentially from any other form of bet. It is *not* investing.

In this chapter we describe:

- the risk to your capital and how to calculate your potential loss depending on the size of your bet
- the tax treatment of any gains or 'winnings'
- what you can bet on
- how to bet on the FTSE 100 index
- the FTSE 100 +04/+05 rule
- how to limit your potential losses
- the importance of the right mental attitude before you make a bet
- the influence of Wall Street on the FTSE 100.

There are two things to remember before anything else.

- **Do not commit yourself for more money than you can afford to lose.**
- **Write off the entire commitment at the time you make the bet.**

If you can live with these two golden rules, and you want to inject some risk and excitement into your life, then spread betting may be for you. It is not a new concept although it has gained popularity in the areas of sport and become quite widely accepted as an alternative to straightforward betting on specific results in football, cricket, rugby football and even on the outcome of general elections. The facility has now extended to cover stockmarket indices, currencies, interest rates, commodities, individual shares and options.

Two important aspects must be mentioned.

- First, you can limit your exposure to loss to as little as £200 per £5 bet which is the minimum.
- Second, any gain or profit you may make is entirely free of all tax including capital gains or income tax.

For the purpose of this book, I shall confine the subject to spread betting on the FTSE 100 index. So before getting into the details of how it works and giving some guidelines as to how to make profits out of betting on this market, I shall explain something about the difference between the 'spot' FTSE 100 and the 'future' FTSE 100.

THE 'SPOT' FTSE 100

As has been described earlier in this book, the FTSE 100 index is a weighted index covering the top 100 shares, measured by market cap-italisation, which are listed and traded on the London Stock Exchange. All through the trading hours every trading day (08.30 to 16.30) the index is displayed on the trading screens and it can alter from moment to moment, and it usually does so. The spot figure is simply a number which alters by larger amounts when the shares which have a heavier weighting are traded than when those with a lower weighting are bought or sold, and it is shown to one decimal point. For example, 4230.8 might be displayed on the screen. There is no underlying value to this index, nor is there any asset backing to the figure. It is just a way of measuring the level of the market for the shares which form a constituent part of the FTSE 100 index and if the buyers outweigh the sellers, the index will go up. If the sellers outweigh the buyers, then the index will fall. Shares traded which have a very large market capitalisation will have a disproportionate affect on the FTSE, so that any movement in the index is not really representative of the market as a whole. Nevertheless, quite a lot of attention is paid to the level of this index.

> 'Spread betting has now extended to cover stockmarket indices, currencies, interest rates, commodities, individual shares and options.'

If, during the day, the bulk of the trading takes place in the financial sector (in shares such as the banks), or Glaxo Wellcome, Smith Kline Beecham, Shell, BP, or any of the other heavyweights, and if the preponderance of the trade is with the buyers, then the rise in the FTSE will be fairly meaningless as far as any significant change in value of the rest of the constituents of the FTSE 100. This is an important point and you will see why when we come to look at ways of making money out of spread betting.

So in essence, what you are doing is to bet whether you think that the index is going to go up or down from the moment you make the bet. Thus you either make an *upbet* or a *downbet* depending upon your view of the future of the market.

THE 'FUTURES' FTSE 100

In the futures and options market, you can invest in FTSE 100 futures in just the same way as any other future whether it be in stocks or shares or currencies, etc. I mention it here because there is a relationship between the spot index (also called the cash price) and the futures index which you should bear in mind. As its name suggests, the futures market reflects the views of investors as to where they think the price of an underlying share might be in three, six or nine months. In just the same way, the FTSE 100 futures will reflect market assessment of the level of the index over the same periods. *All futures prices are expressed in whole numbers. No decimal places.*

As a rule of thumb, the futures price for the FTSE 100 should be about 18 points above the spot price. This is known as the 'fair value'. If the disparity is more than this amount, then it is a sign that the investors believe that the spot figure is too low and they expect it to rise to an 18 point difference. If the disparity is less than 18 points, then the investors expect the spot figure to drop until the margin has come back to a difference of about 18 points. This is not a hard and fast rule but it is a very useful guide to the opinions of the investors or traders in the futures market.

HOW SPREAD BETTING WORKS

There are two firms who will make prices for spread bets, I.G. Index and City Index. The prices which they will quote are based upon the futures price of the subject of the bet, not the spot price, and the values are quoted in whole numbers. The size of the bet varies with each firm. I.G. Index demands a minimum bet of £10 per point in the FTSE, whereas City Index demands £5 per point.

The futures market is divided into four quarters, January to March, April to June, July to September and October to December. You can select a period of three, six or nine months for your bet to run, and the prices which you will be quoted will vary for each one at the time of the quote. However your bet must run from the date that you make it up to the account day of the period which you have chosen. If, for example, you decided to have a bet in February for the account ending in March, the time available for your bet to mature would be less than three months. If you opted for a bet to run until the end of June, then your bet would have under six months to go before maturity. If you have not closed out your bet by the end of the period you have chosen, the bet will be shut down automatically and your position will crystallise so that you will either owe or be owed money.

Now let us take an example. Suppose the FTSE 100 spot value in June were 3720, you might be quoted a spread of 3750 to 3760 for the September FTSE, i.e., for the three-month period.

Let us assume that you think that the index is going to rise by the end of September to a figure high enough to make the futures price go up during that period, because that is what the spread betting firm is using to lay off your bet, then you would place an upbet and the starting point for you would be 3760. This does not mean that the spot value has to rise to 3760, it does mean that the futures level has to rise sufficiently to raise the price at which you can close out the bet. It must be in excess of 3760 before you make any money. For the purpose of this example, suppose that the FTSE 100 did not move at all during the period, and that the quote remained unaltered because the futures price had not moved, then you would be closed out at 3750. This exercise would have resulted in a loss of 10 points (3760 –3750 = 10) which would cost you £100 (10 points @ £10 per point).

On the other hand, if, during the period, your premise was correct and the FTSE had risen, the quote would have followed suit and be standing at, say, 3780 to 3790 so that by closing out at 3780 you would have made a gain of £100.

You do not have to hold the bet for any longer than you want. You could close out the bet five minutes after you have made it if you so desired and this facility forms the main plank of suggestions as to how to win at spread betting.

> **Remember that whilst any gains are completely free from tax because they are classified as winnings from betting, losses can not be offset against profits arising from the realisation of other investments.**

Now that you have digested what the FTSE is, and understood both the difference and the relationship between the spot and future, let me show you how to make money at the game.

The FTSE 100 +04/+05 Rule

I once knew someone who had spent several years studying the opening tick at 08.35 on the FTSE 100. He had no experience in the stockmarket, neither did he have any knowledge of fundamental or technical analysis in the marketplace, nor any interest in such finer techniques. He just followed the first tick on the FTSE 100 and realised that +04 /+05 occurred on a regular basis. He just felt that the market would provide eight such signals during each 20 day trading month and that one should be able to make money when such a pattern appeared.

■ **EXAMPLE**

As I have said, the market opens in London at 08.30 every morning, Monday to Friday. So as an example, let us take the two weeks beginning 14 and 21 April 1997. On the 16th at the end of the trading day, the FTSE spot had closed at 4317. On the 17 it opened at 4328. It progressed as follows:

4328 … 29 … 30 … 31 … 32 … 31 … 32 … 33 … 34 … 32 … 31 … 30 … 28 … 27 … 26 … … … 4300 (low for the day)

The rule says that if the FTSE spot rises after the opening by +04/+05 ticks you should **sell**, i.e., place a **downbet**.

If the FTSE 100 falls after the opening by +04/+05 ticks you should **buy**, i.e., place an **upbet**.

So in this case, the FTSE rose from 4328 to 4334 – +6 ticks – and then fell back to its opening figure of 4328 *at which point you would have placed a downbet*. It continued to fall by a further 28 ticks, which at £10 per tick would have grossed £280 less the amount of the spread.

On April 22 at the end of the trading day, the FTSE spot had closed at 4365. On April 23 it opened at 4400 and it progressed as follows:

4400 ... 02 ... 05 ... 03 ... 02 ... 00 ... 4399 ... 98 ... 97 ... ... 4387 (low for the day) ... 88 ... 94 ... 88 ... ... 4420 (high for the day)

In this case, the FTSE rose from 4400 to 4405 – +5 ticks – and then fell back to its opening figure of 4400 at which point you would have placed another downbet. It continued to fall by a further 13 ticks.

Now this little exercise is quite easy to understand, and very simple to follow and execute profitably. However there is more to it than that.

The traders on the floor apply the Fibonacci principles which I have described in the previous chapter, and the part which is the most pertinent is that concerning support and resistance levels.

If you look at the example shown above for the second day's trading, you will see that the FTSE 100 index rose from an opening figure of 4400 to 4405. So the first resistance level was 4405. Then it fell to 4387 and bounced back up to 4420.

Thus 4387 became a support level and the FTSE did not fall below this figure. In fact it penetrated the resistance level of 4405 to close at a high of 4420.

How to open an account

You do not need to send money to open an account. There are two types of account, a standard account and a deposit account.

A standard account

If you open a standard account, you send a cash deposit on the day you open a bet. It will pay you to shop around to find the best terms for the business which you intend doing. Each broker publishes terms and conditions and each one establishes a deposit limit depending upon the item on which you choose to bet. The deposit requirement is expressed as so many times the bet size (the deposit factor). Sometimes the deposit factor may not be charged in full for two bets running concurrently. For example, if you had a straddle where you had an upbet on the FTSE for one month and a downbet on it for another month.

A credit account

Subject to satisfactory arrangements on both sides, you can open a credit account which eliminates the need to transfer cash immediately in the event that you want to place further bets, or if the need for a margin call should arise while a bet is still open.

Spread betting allows you to gear up your capital because it involves a much smaller outlay than trading directly in the futures and options markets. For example, the minimum bet on the FTSE is £5, whereas on the London Financial Futures Exchange (LIFFE) one lot, which is the minimum, is £25.

In addition, spread betting allows you to place a limit on the amount which you can lose unlike investing directly in futures and options. Bearing in mind the fact that the market can move extremely fast in either direction, unless you watch the futures prices all the time during market hours, you could find that your FTSE future has lost much more money than you envisaged, whilst an equivalent spread bet would have been closed out automatically at a price which meant that your loss was both predetermined and acceptable.

It is important to remember that if you decide to operate on the basis of a stop-loss limit, it is probable that the spread of the quote will be wider. Such bets are called '*controlled risk bets*'.

The bets are dependent upon the broker's quotation moving up or down by an amount sufficient to trigger the buy or sell instruction built in to the controlled risk structure. They are not triggered by the movement of the FTSE 100 index. You must satisfy yourself that you understand completely the rules by which the broker works before you decide to open negotiations and start committing yourself and your money to spread betting. If you have any reservations or doubts about his methods, ask questions until you are satisfied that you fully understand what it is that you are letting yourself in for. Otherwise don't get involved.

MENTAL ATTITUDE

At the beginning of this chapter I said that you should not risk spread betting if you can not afford to lose any money, and that you should write off the entire amount which you *could* lose at the time you make a bet.

But there is a further tip which is well worth bearing in mind, particularly if you decide to swim in this pool on a regular basis. It can become addictive very easily, and a few early successes can give you a feeling of euphoria which may well begin to cloud your judgement. I know someone who makes a living out of spread betting, but he has had many years of experience working in the market on the trading floor and he knows exactly how the futures markets work. The aspect which might appear to be somewhat surprising is, however, an important piece of advice. *Don't deal if you are not in the mood.* It is important that your mental attitude is right and that your approach is uncluttered by distractions or doubts about the market and the external influences such as what may be happening on Wall Street or any imminent economic changes which could have a sudden and dramatic effect on London.

> 'If you have reservations or doubts about his methods, ask questions until you are satisfied that you fully understand what it is that you are letting yourself in for.'

There are days when I, as a stockbroker, have neutral feelings about the market and its general direction, even though I am sitting watching the screens all day, and experience has taught me that when this occurs the best thing to do is to leave the market alone. Unless there is some specific reason for dealing when the market gives one the impression that the whole thing is a non-event and seems to be waiting to make up its mind where it is going next, my advice to my clients is to do nothing and to wait and see. Now this does not matter when one is investing for growth because to hold back from a commitment for a few days will not make any material difference to the target profit to be achieved. If, by so doing it means that the price at which a share is bought is a penny or two higher than it was a day or so previously, it is not going to matter as far as the overall profit is concerned.

But when you are exposing your capital to very short-term risk with the possibility that you can make or lose quite a lot of money within a matter of minutes, you need to have all your wits about you and to have a positive and enthusiastic attitude to what you are doing.

TIP   **Don't forget that you are not going to win every time**. If that were possible, everyone would spend their time playing in this risky game. Probably some bright technician would design a computer program to place the bets and set the controlled risk limits for you so that you could spend your time fishing or playing golf or whatever is your fancy while the machine made money for you. Would that it were possible. But so far it is not, so it is most important that you give yourself the maximum chance of winning and you will not do this if your mood is neutral or negative.

THE INFLUENCE OF WALL STREET ON THE FTSE 100

To understand how Wall Street or the American stockmarkets have an effect on the London market, it is necessary to explain something about timing.

The London Stock Exchange opens at 08.30 Monday to Friday and closes at 16.30 each day. The New York markets open at 14.30 and close at 22.30 London time. Thus they are continuing to trade for six hours after the London Stock Exchange has shut. Now none of this would make any difference, were it not for the fact that investment in shares is now carried out on a global basis. There are plenty of investors, both private and institutional, on both sides of the Atlantic, who buy and sell shares which are listed and traded on each others' stock exchanges. Consequently, for one reason or another, the closing level of the main indices for both markets can and often does have an influence on the opening level and immediate direction of each other. You will realise that if the Dow Jones closes at the end of a trading day at a considerably higher level than it opened, it will have done so while the London market was shut. Thus when the London market opens next day, it will do so with the knowledge that Wall Street was bullish and the sentiment will probably be positive.

TIP **Since Wall Street is trading for six hours after the London market has closed, it pays to know what sector of the market in New York was the subject of interest and influence on the *Standard and Poor* 500 index later on each day**. The Dow Jones index covers the top 30 companies by market capitalisation; the Standard and Poor index covers the top 500 and is considered to be more representative. Any major movement in the closing price of a sector in New York is likely to be reflected in London in early trading on the following day. If for example, a rumour was started that interest rates in America might go up shortly, or the chairman of the Federal Reserve Bank makes a speech which instigates or fuels the rumour, then there will probably be some heavy trading in the financial sector. Consequently the same sector in London will be the subject of considerable scrutiny by the market makers and the fund managers. This fact may well mean that the FTSE 100 index opens at a substantially different level to that at which it closed the day before.

If, in early trading in London, the bulk of the activity is concentrated in the financial sector, as one would expect under these conditions, then you would expect the FTSE to move substantially more than usual because the 'weighting' of the financial shares in the index is much higher than it is for most of the rest of the constituent shares.

Thus, if there has been heavy selling in New York, you can expect the FTSE to drop by quite a lot; if there was heavy buying then the opposite would apply. The other sector which exerts abnormal influence is the oil sector.

To be successful at spread betting on the FTSE 100, you have to be fully informed about the closing prices on Wall Street for the day before and have access to real time prices from the London Stock Exchange every day and be ready to place your bet by 08.30 every morning. Any later than that and you have missed the boat.

SUMMARY

In this chapter we have investigated spread betting with particular emphasis on the following points:

- the risks involved in spread betting and the amount of potential capital loss even on the minimum bet of £5 per point;
- the sense in limiting your risk of loss;
- how to bet on the FTSE 100 index and make money regularly using the +04/+05 rule;
- the two ways to open a betting account;
- how important it is not to bet if you do not feel 'in the mood';
- why it pays you to be as fully informed as possible about the sectors which were being traded most heavily on Wall Street the previous day.

PART

INVESTING

INTRODUCTION TO PART 2

This part is devoted to investing as opposed to trading. At the beginning of the book, I stressed the need to separate the two functions and the fact that you have to have a completely different approach and mental attitude to each one. This part explains how to be a long-term investor, and tells you in detail why your approach must be the opposite of that for trading. It covers the following aspects of your approach to investing:

- why research is so important
- where to find the data you need for research
- how to choose the right shares
- how to analyse the *five* essential indices in a company's accounts
- the influence of politics on the market
- how to use Trust laws to avoid inheritance tax and how to use insurance to cover inheritance tax liabilities.

THE VITAL NEED FOR RESEARCH

INTRODUCTION

In the first part of the book I explained that a trader does not really care whether the company he chooses to invest in is making widgets or war ships, or whether its market capitalisation is large, medium or small. Short-term performance is all that is of interest, and providing he or she can find a share where the price is volatile and the trend is upwards, then there is a very good chance that adequate profits can be made. Regular 'in and out' trading.

In this chapter, we describe the reasons why there is a vital need for research for the long-term investor *before* buying anything. They are as follows:

- risk evaluation
- market direction
- the right time to buy.

Long-term investing is a totally different ball game from short-term trading. Here the object is to invest in a share *and leave it alone* for as long as it is meeting its target for growth, which should be for at least one year and probably for longer than that.

I am assuming that, in this context, not only is the prime requirement of the long-term investor to buy shares for capital growth, but also that income is of secondary importance, and I have completely discounted giving any consideration to it here. In my book *Be Your Own Stockbroker*, I demonstrated how to assemble a portfolio for income and growth, as well as how to construct one for income alone. Whilst I am aware that everyone's requirements are different, most people want to build up the value of their capital or, at the very least, to protect it against the ravages of inflation. So this book is concentrating on the ways in which you can increase your wealth with the minimum risk of loss.

> '... the object is to invest in a share *and leave it alone* for as long as it is meeting its target for growth...'

Once you have made your decision to buy a particular share, the last thing you want to have to do is to sell it before it has made a profit. Money, like any other asset should work to 'earn its keep', and you want it to make sufficient profit before you incur the costs of selling and buying another one.

For long-term investing, it is vital to ensure that you cover every area where things might go wrong in the future in any company whose shares you are considering buying. After all it is your money that is at risk and you have only got yourself to blame if you have not been sufficiently diligent in ensuring that you have done everything possible to evaluate the risks before you decide to invest.

If you were going to buy a house, you would be crazy not to have a survey done on the structure and fabric of the building. But if the results of the survey showed no material defects and you went ahead with the competition of the purchase without investigating local government planning intentions, or bothering to find out if the property was in the middle of an aircraft glide path, or if the surrounding area was liable to flooding or some other potential threat to your investment, let alone your peace of mind, you would not feel very clever.

> **The more research you do the easier it is to evaluate the risks and consequently the better your judgement will be.**

Before you get daunted by the whole concept of researching companies, and wondering where to start, remember that much of it boils down to commonsense and experience. The former is something everyone has if they choose to use it, the latter will come with time. Research can be split into two general areas of activity.

CURRENT AFFAIRS

The first one comes under the heading of 'current affairs' which is obtained by reading newspapers and generally having an interest in what is going on in the world. For example, there was an item on the news recently about a new drug which would be of considerable aid to those unfortunate enough to suffer from Altzheimer's disease. My immediate reaction was to wonder who manufactures the drug because obviously there will be considerable profits generated from its sale and because the disease is widespread, the demand for the treatment is likely to be large and sustained. Likewise, the announcement by the government that the onus for providing pensions in the future is going to fall more and more on the shoulders of individuals, rather than on the State, is likely to mean that the insurance companies will benefit from an increase of funds under management. Since they make their profits by investing other people's money, the more they have to manage, the greater their profits are likely to be. Pension savings are long-term savings, and therefore the earnings potential of the insurance companies which specialise in pension fund management are likely to increase steadily over many years. If their earnings grow, so will their share price. These are just two examples of applying a bit of lateral thinking to some items of current affairs.

However, by themselves, neither of these two examples should mean that you would rush out and buy shares in all or any of the pharmaceutical or insurance companies without doing much more research. What they *do* show is how everyday items of news can and should alert you to investigate something of interest to see whether there is potential for a long-term investment.

EXPERIENCE

The second one comes under the heading of experience. Before we get down to specific sources of data for you to use, it is worth looking at what makes a company successful or not. The reason for defining these areas is because if you get into the habit of investigating each one and using the categories as a checklist, you will not forget to examine what might be the essential factor which could influence your investment decision. The 'weighting' which you give to each item will vary according to the size of the company, the industrial sector in which it sits, its markets, its management and so on. There is no short cut to teach you the variations in the 'weighting', you will get such ability from experience.

THE MARKET

Let us assume that you have won £500,000 on the pools or the lottery. Further, your aim is to invest the capital for steady growth and you have not got all day and every day to spend watching the share prices. You want to find a number of shares to buy which will do the business for you and your objective is to change them as infrequently as possible. You start with the market first, and only when you have satisfied yourself that you know where it is going do you concentrate on individual shares.

How and where to start

The first thing to do is to set an overall target for capital growth for your money. It would be foolish to expect to double the values within 12 months. It would be equally foolish to have no target at all, although it never ceases to amaze me how many people simply ignore the performance of their portfolio altogether and wonder why a significant part of it does so badly.

The first thing to establish is what the market *as a whole* is doing and whether the trend overall is upward or downward. Thus the first piece of research is to establish the *annual rate of growth or decline* for the market generally.

Market direction

There are several indices which are published daily showing the performance of different sections of the market, as well as the whole market. As we have said earlier on, there are over 3,300 shares listed on the London Stock Exchange, so there has to be some method of segregating them into convenient groups. This is done by the market capitalisation measurement. The most frequently used one is the FTSE 100. This category includes the 100 shares whose share price multiplied by the number of their ordinary shares in issue shows the greatest value. For example, Boots has a market capitalisation in excess of £6,200 million. Capita Group, a company with a history of sustained and substantial growth in both profits and share price has a market capitalisation of £380 million. Capita Group is not included in the FTSE 100. If safety is to be measured by the size of market capitalisation, then Capita Group would feature some way down the list. However, this measurement is only one of the yardsticks to be used. The other groups are the FTSE 250, the FTSE 350 and the FT-SE All-Share index. With the exception of the last one, these groupings are measurements of the market capitalisation of each company within its group.

There are times, particularly in a bull market, when you will see that the FTSE 100 has moved up by a lesser amount than either the 250 or the 350. A long term investor should ignore such short-term variations.

It is generally accepted that the larger the market capitalisation, the safer the company. The reasoning behind this is that a company with a big capital base is better able to withstand a downturn in the economic climate than one with a smaller capital base. Nevertheless this is only one factor to be considered albeit an important one.

So you will need to look at the trend of the groups over the last two years at the very minimum to establish a benchmark against which to set your targets. Let us suppose that the FTSE 100 index has risen by 6 per cent per annum for the last two years. Your target will be to beat that figure because if you cannot do so, you might as well put your money into a 'tracker' fund which simply invests in the shares which form part of the FTSE 100 and let someone else do all the work for you. If the FTSE 100 has risen by 6 per cent, then some of the shares within it will have risen by considerably more than that figure. Let us assume that some have risen by as much as 25 per cent over the same period. You will see therefore, that the most you could aim for would be a growth rate of 25 per cent as a target for the next year, but you would probably be very lucky to achieve that figure if you include a demand for safety within your parameters. The reason I say that is because in most cases share prices tend to rise in a series of steps. After a substantial uplift in value they generally go though a period of consolidation before the next upward movement so if a small number of the FTSE 100 shares achieved a growth rate considerably in excess of the average, not only will they be unlikely to sustain it, but also it will probably be extremely difficult to find others which will match their performance.

The important thing is to set realistic and achievable targets for your investments and you can only do this by researching the histories of the group in which the share is included as well as that of the individual share price itself. There is an adage in the market that quality will always look after you, and I strongly recommend that you follow it. I should allocate at least 60 per cent of your capital to investments in shares in the FTSE 100 list, and depending upon your age, income and family inheritance planning, maybe an even higher percentage should be invested in such shares.

When you analyse the performance of the FTSE 250 and 350, you will probably find that the FTSE 100 has risen at a faster rate than the other two. This is because there is always a greater demand for shares in larger companies with bigger market capitalisation since investors equate safety with size.

However, sometimes individual shares in smaller companies will outperform the market by a considerable amount. Factors such as tax incentives to the manufacturing industry or favourable exchange rates can boost the order books of smaller companies and this reflects in their profits more quickly than it might do in larger ones.

> 'There is an adage in the market that quality will always look after you, and I strongly recommend that you follow it.'

The historic record of rise or fall of the market in general and of individual shares in particular must be looked at in relation to outside events at the time. There is always a reason for any movement and you must find out the reasons why such movements occurred. The movements of the market are the manifestations of fear or greed. Markets tend to drop faster than they rise, and this is a lesson in itself. If war suddenly becomes a possibility, markets react badly. If there is an anticipation of a substantial rise in interest rates in Britain, or the USA or Germany, the London market will get the shakes. It is often said that if Wall Street sneezes, London catches a bad cold. Anything which is thought might push the price of oil up worldwide would knock the market even if the fears proved unfounded and the reaction was only temporary. The main lessons to be absorbed by the investor who is relatively new to the game are:

- fear of the unknown and its possible effects will always knock the market downwards;
- the market always over reacts and such dramatic falls can produce very good buying opportunities.

Why have I introduced these two elements into the section concerned with research? Because by looking at the historical record of the market over the years you can measure the effects of such events when they occurred in the past and you can evaluate both the amount of the drop in prices and the time it took the market to recover from the reversals.

But the market will move in an erratic fashion in just the same way as share prices do on a daily or weekly basis and the investor should be aware of how to judge whether the market as a whole is oversold or overbought. If it is oversold, then the natural reaction is for it to turn upwards, and if it is overbought, then the next movement will almost certainly be downwards.

How to assess the market

There are many different theories as to how to recognise the current state of the market and whether it is oversold or overbought, and people spend their whole working day trying to forecast exactly the next move and to quantify it. Books have been written on the subject and the financial Press publishes the opinions of economists and investment 'gurus' every day of the week. If anyone was really infallible, they would have made so much money that they could have bought the country, let alone a few country houses, and they certainly would not write about how it was done. Nevertheless, there are several pointers which can be used and those, coupled with common-sense, are all that can be used to make intelligent guesses. The best that you can hope for is to eliminate as much of the unknown as possible so that you reduce the area of chance, or luck, or whatever you want to call it, to the minimum.

One of the ways to establish the state of the market is to look at the futures and options market. A traded option gives the buyer the right to buy or sell a share at a date in the future at a price which is fixed at the time of purchase. The futures and option market indicates the level to which it is anticipated the stockmarket will rise or fall in the fairly short-term.

You will see from the graph of the market shown in Figure 7.1 just how much the values of investment have risen, particularly in the latter years. Over 20 plus years, the trend has been upward.

The right time to buy

We have explained that a long-term investor is not concerned with short term volatility of a share price. However, there are right and wrong times to buy a share. The first things to look at are the 'high' and 'low' records for each individual share and the dates on which the dividends are payable.

Examples of 'highs' and 'lows' are given in Figure 7.2. You will see that they are shown monthly, and the data is taken from the *Financial Times*. Whilst this is an interesting though brief overview, you will get much more detail from a chart showing you the actual intermediate movements. If you refer back to Figure 2.1, which is the chart for Boots for the five years ending 16 November 1996, you will see that if you had bought the share in January 1994, it would have taken until about March 1996 before the price had returned to the level which you paid. In January 1994, you would have had nothing else to go on other than the performance up to that point. Then it was at an all-time high over the period in question. Although the trend was rising rapidly up to that date, it would have been foolish under any circumstances to go in at the top. This chart shows a classic example of the share price movement repeating itself because from mid 1992 onwards until January 1994 (and in fact subsequently on regular occasions), a substantial rise in the price has been followed by a falling trend of quite considerable amounts. Nevertheless the share certainly

Fig 7.1 Graph of the market from 1954

(Source: *Financial Times*)

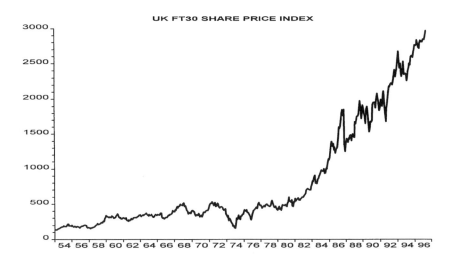

UK FT30 SHARE PRICE INDEX

Fig 7.2 Examples of 'highs' and 'lows'

(Source: *Financial Times*)

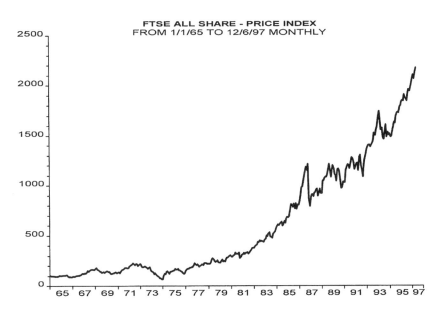

FTSE ALL SHARE - PRICE INDEX
FROM 1/1/65 TO 12/6/97 MONTHLY

145

qualifies as a 'blue chip' and anyone who bought at around 450p has been well rewarded.

Timing is essential, as it is in most actions in life, but in the case of buying shares, there is a lot of recorded data which very often can be used to enhance your profits if you use it properly.

SUMMARY

In this chapter we have stressed the need for research. We have explained that:

- commonsense and experience are the best bases to start from;
- the more research you do, the better your judgement will be;
- market direction must be established before committing yourself;
- the right time to buy is when the market is oversold.

SOURCES OF DATA FOR RESEARCH

INTRODUCTION

In this chapter, we examine the question of where to find the data you need for research. Nowadays there is so much information published about companies, and their products, markets, management, profits and so on that it is bewildering to say the least to know where to start. Also, for the investor with limited time to spare for research, it helps to know which items are important and which ones can safely be ignored.

In this chapter we look at the following sources of data for research:

● the Press including financial journals
● Extel cards
● stockbrokers' circulars.

The first thing to do is to choose the sector which you think is likely to be 'set fair' for the next two or three years in terms of economic growth. For example, at the end of 1978 and to some extent during 1979, the economists were all telling us that the world manufacturing industries were in recession. This statement was a general one, and there were manufacturing companies around the globe which were thriving and growing, but there were more companies with few orders on their books than there were those working to full capacity. The bell-wether share for the global manufacturing industry is probably RTZ. It supplies most of the metals and ores required in manufacturing from bauxite (for aluminium) to zinc (for coatings for steel). RTZ's range of products includes tungsten and copper which are universally employed in the manufacture of electronic goods. So an analysis of the sales figures and the chairman's statement with particular regard to his comments on the future expectations of orders and expansion of the various extractive and processing companies owned by RTZ will give you a fair indication of what the future level of manufacturing industry is likely to be. Falling orders mean a deepening recession, rising orders mean that the nadir has been passed, and you can expect the whole industry to start to climb out of recession.

In the same way, ICI paints division used to be a good indicator of the building and construction industry, although this is not quite so accurate nowadays as it once was. You would monitor the same items in the accounts for Tarmac, RMC, Redlands or Laing (J).

You need to bone up on your knowledge of the leaders in the various sectors and use all the information which is available from reading their *Reports and Accounts* to give yourself a benchmark against which to measure the potential of other companies.

THE PRESS

The best places to find opinions concerning the potential future growth prospects or dangers which might affect the share price adversely are the *Financial Times* (Saturday issue if nothing else), *Daily Telegraph*, *The Times*, (Sunday issue at least) and the *Investors Chronicle*. There is a wealth of informed comment in these papers and, with practice, it will not take you long to scan through the few columns which will give you a good basic understanding of the fears and aspirations of various sectors of the market. Your interest will be aroused by an article about a sector, and it is from that starting point that you should begin your more detailed research.

> 'Falling orders mean a deepening recession, rising orders mean that the nadir has been passed, and you can expect the whole industry to start to climb out of the recession.'

EXTEL CARDS

I know that I have repeatedly referred to Extel card information in this book, and I make no apology for so doing. The data contained in them are invaluable in many ways.

First, you can see at a glance from the data for the last five years the key features which are the most important for your quick analysis of the progress of the company and measurement of the management's ability to perform. It saves having to work out the details from separate issues of the *Profit & Loss Accounts* and *Balance Sheets* from which the data is obtained.

Second, with a little practice you can isolate the financial data which will show the probable reason for a decline in earnings or profits. Thus, you can go to the heart of an anomaly very quickly and confine your questions to the one or two areas which have resulted in an abnormal dip or jump in the earnings or profit progress.

These are all tools for your trade. They will help you to concentrate on the bits that matter, so that you can satisfy yourself that the share is worth buying, or retaining, after you have found out the answers to the anomalies which they throw up.

STOCKBROKERS' CIRCULARS

Stockbrokers' circulars or newsletters are another useful area for research. There is bound to be a certain amount of selectivity in these, because whoever writes them will almost certainly have their own particular favourites and prejudices. However, experience will tell you whether you put a lot or a little faith in the ones you receive, depending upon the accuracy of their recommendations which you can judge for yourself after watching the progress of each one of them for a time. The added advantage of receiving these newsletters is that you can discuss the comments with the analyst who wrote them for further insight as to why they like or dislike the share. You can ask the broking firms to put you on to their regular mailing list without any obligation.

CHECKING THE FACTS

What you should *not* do is to buy a share blind simply because someone has given you a tip. There is an old saying in the market: 'Where there's a tip, there's a tap'. This means that when someone whispers in your ear that you should be buying the XYZ company at, say, 50p, it is because he has bought them some time ago at 20p and is keen to boost investor demand, so that when he sells his holding it does not depress the price for him. I think that the relevance of that old adage has largely disappeared in today's markets because it really applied to dealers on the floor of the Stock Exchange, but it is still worth remembering when you are considering some of the really speculative mining shares, for example.

The greed factor will always be present in every investor's make-up. The essential thing is to recognise its existence and to double-check the 'facts' that you are being fed. The more responsible the paper reporting a 'find' the better, but even those which guard their reputations for probity most carefully cannot guard against fraudulent operators. Recently the *Financial Times* published an article about the ruinous lure of fool's gold. Quoting Mark Twain during the 1849 gold rush, when he said, 'A mine is a hole in the ground with a liar standing next to it', the piece went on to expose some of the more recent examples of short-lived boom and bust investment situations where the public saw the share prices rise meteorically only to collapse very soon afterwards. The list includes Timbuktu Gold, Poseidon and its supposed massive nickel deposits, Cartaway, and more recently Bre-X, which had claimed to have found the world's biggest gold deposits in Indonesia. As technology has progressed and improved, so has the ability of unscrupulous operators. Samples of drilling can be injected with minute quantities of the precious metals to ensure that independent geologists find positive traces of their existence, thus ensuring confirmation of the fraudulent claims.

It is an unpleasant fact that as time goes on, the investor has to adopt a much more cynical and questioning approach to any claims which might appear to make him or her rich quickly. There are opportunities to find shares which are standing at very low prices and which do find large reserves of valuable commodities, and whose share price leaps when the news is released, but these are few and far between and the admonition '*caveat emptor*' was never more appropriate than for these types of investments.

It will always pay you to concentrate on getting to know as much as you can about the business of two or three sectors and keeping the bulk of your investments within those areas. If you follow this advice, you will limit the amount of research required and you will begin to find the most effective sources of information concerning the companies which are listed within those sectors. The more you can become an expert on your selected investment areas, the more you will reduce the areas of the unknown quantities and thus reduce the risk. Commonsense will dictate what is reasonable to expect by way of growth in the sector. What you are trying to do is to find one or more of the constituent members of the sector which is most likely to outperform the rest, and to this extent, the more information you can gather, the more you are likely to succeed.

> 'Concentrate on getting to know as much as you can about the business of two or three sectors and keep the bulk of your investments within those areas.'

SUMMARY

In this chapter we have demonstrated in detail the following points:

- the valuable information which is conveyed in the quality papers;
- the importance of finding out as much as possible about the history of the management, the market for the company's products and the competition for any company reviewed in the Press.

HOW TO SELECT THE RIGHT SHARES AT THE RIGHT TIME

INTRODUCTION

The average investor, when starting to build a portfolio, is faced with a huge choice of different shares from which to choose. This chapter is devoted to explaining how you set about selecting the right shares for your own particular objectives and the right time to buy them. You may think that this chapter should have appeared earlier on in the book: but I have not done so for a reason. In the previous chapters I have deliberately followed a sequence which emphasises the need for understanding research and demonstrating that it is a very big subject. Unless you tackle the task of research in a structured way, you will only scratch the surface and you will end up either with insufficient knowledge over a wide range of shares, or you will become reliant on the opinions of others, in which case the whole object of keeping control over the strategic planning of your investments will be lost.

In this chapter we shall show you:

- how to establish a fair value for a share
- how to recognise when a share is expensive and when it is cheap
- how to gauge market sentiment
- how to do your own local market research.

The objective is to demonstrate the need for you to start by learning as much as possible about a relatively small segment of the market which you can cope with in a limited time. After that, you can expand your scope and add to the size of the segment as you feel sufficiently confident and more experienced in finding and assimilating information quickly.

CONSTRUCTING A PORTFOLIO

So in order to find out how to choose the right shares, let us first define what we mean by 'right'.

It goes without saying that we are aiming to achieve the following objectives:

- to make sufficient profit *each year on each investment* to beat the Retail Price Index;
- to keep any switching of investments to the absolute minimum to contain dealing costs;
- to minimise the risk of loss of capital.

Now these objectives may not seem to be very exciting, but excitement should not be part of any long-term investor's expectations. You get the buzz from trading together with the commensurate risks involved. The most successful portfolios I have seen invested for the long term are those which have contained a relatively few shares in the leading quality companies whose business represents the core of the wealth creation of the economy. Such portfolios are eminently safe and over the years will grow happily without being disturbed. Nevertheless, depending upon how many years back you go in order to measure the growth, you must re-evaluate your selections fairly regularly to ensure that there has not been a fundamental change in economic conditions which could jeopardise your whole strategy.

> '... in order to find out how to choose the right shares, let us first define what we mean by 'right'.'

■ EXAMPLE

Let me give you an example. In the first half of the 20th century, there was almost no inflation. This meant that house prices remained static, or if they did increase, it was by very small amounts and usually such increases in value were brought about by social rather than economic reasons. The absence of inflation meant also that wages remained undisturbed with the result that the only thing that affected the price of finished goods was any increase in the cost of raw materials. If the price of coffee beans went up because of a bad harvest, then that item alone would affect the price of coffee. So the only way to ensure that your capital grew was to speculate in risky ventures, or to invest it into government debt, spend less of the income you received, save the rest and buy more gilts. Safety was the watchword of the greater part of the investing public and this was a legacy from Victorian times. It was inconceivable that the government would fail to pay the interest on the due dates, or, more importantly that the amount of interest payable on any gilt would not be enough to provide for living expenses and allow the investor to save regularly if a reasonable amount of capital was involved. In real terms, not a great deal of capital was needed compared with present circumstances.

I still come across portfolios which are so constructed, and they are usually ones which belong to people of fairly advanced years who inherited them. Their benefactors had stressed the dangers of investing in equities and the present owners have been too frightened to change their investments, usually because of a total ignorance of economic reality. The consequence is, of course, that their capital values have eroded to pitiful sums and their income is desperately inadequate for the current cost of living.

Such changes in market and economic conditions evolve gradually, of course, but it is well worth bearing in mind that the variety of investment vehicles is increasing almost daily and the ability to measure safety for capital conservation is becoming less and less easy to determine.

■ EXAMPLE

To take one example, there are now more unit trust funds registered in London and actively inviting investments than there are shares listed on the London Stock Exchange. Quite apart from the safety factor, it is impossible to understand how all of them can beat the index. After all, the objective must be to do better than the average, and if the index represents the average, then not only are the results of most of them likely to prove unsatisfactory, but the protection against erosion of the capital by an upsurge in inflation or from a general downturn in the market must be in serious doubt. This dramatic growth in the numbers of unit trusts is a manifestation of the changing attitudes to investment in recent times.

If you do *not* want to be bothered with managing your own portfolio, and at the same time your prime requirement is to safeguard your capital as far as possible, then you should invest in one of the leading

161

tracker funds which will simply mirror the market index. Don't forget though that there will be an annual charge levied on the fund because someone else is doing the work of selection and monitoring and switching the underlying investments for you from time to time. You can do this yourself just as easily without paying extra for the privilege.

One of the best truisms of investing on the stock market is that quality will always look after you. The way in which the FTSE indices are constructed gives you a clue as to how to pick your shares.

LARGER COMPANIES

The largest companies in each sector, measured by market capitalisation, carry a 'weighting factor' which is greater than that given to smaller companies. For example, let us look at the oil sector as we did earlier in the book. This is mainly dominated by Shell and BP whose market capitalisation is considerably larger than those of any of the smaller exploration or agency companies (see Figure 9.1). Any movement of the share price of Shell or BP will have a greater effect on the sector value, and consequently on the FTSE, than would be the case if one or more of the smaller companies' share price were to move by the same amount (see Figure 9.2). You will realise from this that an upward movement of the FTSE will not necessarily be reflected in a similar upward movement in the share price of one of the smaller companies, and it is this point which is very important to bear in mind when selecting a share in any given sector.

To give you a simple example of the way the weighting factor works, if the share price of a company with a market capitalisation of £1 billion moves up 10p, it will have twice the effect on the FTSE 100 than if the share price of a company with a market capitalisation of £500 million moved up by the same amount.

Another point to remember is that the demand for the shares of such bigger companies is much greater than it is for the smaller ones. The Americans are big buyers of British shares and they will almost

Fig 9.1 The oil sector

(Source: *Financial Times*)

OIL EXPLORATION & PRODUCTION

	Notes	Price	+ or –	1997 high	1997 low	Mkt Cap£m	Yld Gr's	P/E
Abbot Group	🚶♣	**129½**	...	**138½**	113½	**180.0**	1.9	27.5
Alliance Res	♣	**28½**	+4	***85¼**	22½	**8.86**	–	ϕ
Aminex I£	♣	**79½**	...	**85½**	60½	**40.2**	–	ϕ
Aviva Petlm		**29½**	...	**42½**	25½	**9.30**	–	–
Bitech Ptrlm		**116½**	–3½	***140**	75	**30.8**	–	–
Brit Borneo	🚶♣	**1390**	–50	**1542½**	788½	**886.8**	0.7	59.3
Bula Res I£	♣	**1½**	...	**2½**	1½	**24.4**	–	ϕ
Cairn Energy	🚶♣	**482**	–½	***639**	415	**817.0**	–	–
Central Pacific A$	♥	**452½**	–4¼	**527¼**	337¾	**454.0**	–	–
Coplex Resources A$	♥	**20¼**	–1	**22**	11¾	**40.6**	–	–
Dana Petroleum I£	♣	**23¼**	...	**26¼**	14¾	**140.3**	–	–
Dominion Energy		**10**	...	**14¼**	4	**4.71**	–	–
Dragon Oil		**3¼xr**	...	***3½**	1¼	**279.1**	–	ϕ
Edinburgh	🚶♣	**28**	...	**38½**	24¼	**9.77**	1.2	17.4
Warrants		**10½**	...	**17½**	8½	**0.36**	–	–
Emerald Energy	♣	**4¾**	...	**8¼**	3½	**37.8**	–	–
Energy Africa	♣	**303¾**	–½	**327**	202¾	**290.8**	–	–
Enterprise	🚶♣	**715**	–13	**732½**	604	**3,546**	3.0	27.5
Evergreen Res US$	♥	**614¾**	–8¾	**636¼**	423	**57.4**	–	–
Expro Intl	🚶♣	**455xd**	+5	**536½**	433½	**275.3**	2.2	22.5
First Austin Res A$		**17¾**	+½	**22**	12¼	**5.60**	–	–
Fortune	🚶♣n	**15¼**	...	**16¾**	10½	**166.5**	–	59.9
Gaelic Res		**1¼**	...	**1¾**	1	**3.25**	–	–
Gulfstream C$	♥	**474¼**	–5¾	**700½**	474¼	**263.4**	–	–
Hardy Oil & Gas	🚶♣a	**346½**	...	**347½**	264½	**410.6**	0.5	52.1
Intl Pet C$	♥	**278¼**	–¾	**377**	258¾	**115.5**	–	–
Intl Tool & Supply	♣	**6½**	...	**8**	5	**15.8**	–	–
JKX Oil & Gas	♣	**40**	...	***105½**	29	**46.6**	–	–
LASMO	🚶♣N	**266**	–7½	**284**	216½	**2,569**	0.8	–
Ops		**42**	...	**47½**	41	**2.98**	24.7	–
Monument	♣	**86¼**	–¾	***92**	67¼	**603.4**	–	49.0
Oceonics		**19#**	...	***19½**	18½	**8.38**	–	–
Ohio Res C$	♥	**47**	–¼	**67**	40	**4.52**	–	–
Pacrim Energy A$		**4¾**	...	**6½**	4¾	**2.43**	–	–
Pan Pacific A$		**12**	–¼	**12¼**	6	**23.8**	–	–
Pentex Energy	♣	**16**	+½	**27¾**	12¾	**56.0**	6.8	4.1
Pittencrieff Res	🚶♣	**46½**	+1½	**57½**	39	**26.8**	–	15.7
Premier Oil	♣	**47**	–¼	**48¼**	34½	**484.3**	1.5	10.6
Ranger C$		**575¾**	–8	**654**	528¼	**566.8**	3.3	10.5
Schlumberger $		**£79 19/32**	+4 23/32	**£79 19/32**	£59	**19,370**	1.1	–
Seafield Res	♣	**59**	...	**79½**	46½	**40.6**	–	55.9
Soco International		**281½**	+1	**281½**	234½	**138.9**	–	–
Southern Pacific A$	♥	**182**	–7½	***220¾**	142¾	**505.9**	–	–
Stirling Res A$	♥	**5**	...	**5**	3¼	**3.54**	–	–
Sun Resources A$		**13¼**	–¼	**13½**	7½	**2.13**	–	–
Tracer Petroleum C$		**11¾**	–4¼	**23¼**	9½	**4.33**	–	–
Tullow	♣	**90**	...	***103¾**	85	**197.1**	–	ϕ
Tuskar Res I£	‡‡♣	**5**	...	**8¼**	2	**52.3**	–	–
United Energy		**17½**	+½	**24½**	16½	**6.79**	–	8.1
Vanguard Petrlm A$		**19**	–¼	**25**	14¾	**20.3**	–	–
Victoria Petrlm A$		**8½**	+¼	**9**	2¼	**13.3**	–	–
XCL $		**13½**	...	**21½**	12½	**25.5**	–	–
Ser A Cnv Prfd $		**£11¼**	–1/32	**£14 7/16**	£6	**7.26**	–	–

OIL, INTEGRATED

	Notes	Price	+ or –	1997 high	1997 low	Mkt Cap£m	Yld Gr's	P/E
Atlantic Richfield US$		**£43 11/32**	–13/32	***£46 1/32**	£38 9/32	**13,761**	3.9	–
Brit Petroleum	🚶†	**778½xd**	–7½	**792½**	662	**42,265**	3.3	16.4
Burmah Castrol	🚶N	**981½xd**	–4½	**1109**	976	**2,080**	4.7	13.8
Chevron US$		**£44 31/32**	–5/32	**£46 15/16**	£38 7/32	**29,301**	2.8	–
Exxon US$	h	**£38 9/32**	+¼	***£39 5/16**	£28 29/32	**95,077**	2.4	–
KBC Advanced Techs	L	**242½**	...	**264½**	235½	**110.0**	1.7	26.8
Mobil $		**£42⅜**	+1/16	***£43 21/32**	£36 1/32	**33,518**	3.0	–
Norsk Hydro NKr	♣	**£31 11/32**	–5/16	**£35 19/32**	£28 5/16	**7,320**	1.8	10.2
Occidental Petlm $		**£15 7/32**	...	**£16¼**	£13 15/32	**4,581**	3.9	–
Petrofina BFr		**£216⅛**	–1 1/16	**£225 21/32**	£189 7/16	**4,998**	3.0	18.3
Royal Dutch Fl		**£31 7/16**	–3/32	***£32¼**	£25 7/32	**161,753**	2.5	ϕ
Santos A$	♥	**253**	–4½	**264½**	218¼	**1,359**	4.2	–
Shell Transport	🚶♣h	**439½xc**	–3	***449**	329¾	**43,708**	3.5	22.0
7pc Pf		**84¾xd**	–½	**90¾**	83¼	**8.47**	7.2	–
Total B FFr		**£61¼**	–3/16	**£63 17/32**	£46 9/16	**14,773**	1.4	39.0

Figure 9.2 Extract from FTSE Actuaries Industry Sectors

(Source: *Financial Times*)

	Jul 4	Day's chge%	Jul 3	Jul 2	Jul1	Year ago	Div. yld%	Net cover	P/E ratio	Xd adj. ytd	Total Return	1997 High	(date)	1997 Low	(date)	Since Compilation High	(date)	Since Compilation Low	(date)
FTSE 100	4812.8	-0.4	4831.7	4751.4	4728.3	3743.2	3.39	2.04	18.08	91.51	2055.56	4831.7	3/7	4056.6	10/1	4831.7	3/7/97	986.9	23/7/84
FTSE 250	4453.0	-0.5	4475.2	4471.3	4452.5	4367.2	3.72	1.61	20.81	97.16	1864.71	4729.4	11/3	4431.3	30/6	4729.4	11/3/97	1379.4	21/1/86
FTSE 250 ex IT	4451.0	-0.6	4476.5	4473.6	4454.9	4406.9	3.87	1.64	19.61	100.13	1869.35	4773.8	10/3	4434.3	30/6	4773.8	10/3/97	1378.3	21/1/86
FTSE 350	2311.3	-0.4	2320.9	2289.2	2278.3	1884.8	3.45	1.95	18.54	45.15	2017.04	2320.9	3/7	2017.9	2/1	2320.9	3/7/97	664.5	14/1/86
FTSE 350 ex IT	2311.6	-0.4	2321.3	2289.1	2278.3	-	3.48	1.96	18.31	12.70	1034.31	2321.3	3/7	1111.3	9/5	2321.3	3/7/97	1111.3	9/5/97
FTSE 350 Higher Yield	2265.2	-0.4	2274.8	2235.3	2221.5	1800.5	4.62	1.76	15.35	53.62	1675.69	2274.8	3/7	1934.8	2/1	2274.8	3/7/97	100.0	14/12/94
FTSE 350 Lower Yield	2364.7	-0.4	2374.2	2349.3	2340.9	1976.4	2.47	2.25	22.50	36.08	1690.00	2391.5	13/6	2106.2	10/1	2391.5	13/6/97	100.0	14/12/94
FTSE SmallCap	2226.62		2227.19	2226.86	2225.62	2186.10	3.18	1.74	22.58	40.80	1894.04	2374.20	12/3	2178.29	2/1	2374.20	12/3/97	1363.79	31/12/92
FTSE SmallCap ex IT	2198.22	-0.1	2199.38	2199.94	2200.17	2187.23	3.44	1.83	19.91	43.81	1885.92	2382.36	13/3	2190.80	2/1	2382.36	13/3/97	1363.79	31/12/92
FTSE All-Share	2260.61	-0.4	2269.36	2240.42	2230.43	1868.75	3.43	1.94	18.76	43.95	2002.25	2269.36	3/7	1989.78	2/1	2269.36	3/7/97	61.92	13/12/74
FTSE All-Share ex IT	2260.68	-0.4	2269.73	2240.06	2230.08	-	3.47	1.96	18.39	12.60	1029.67	2269.73	3/7	1085.67	9/5	2269.73	3/7/97	1085.67	9/5/95

■ FTSE Actuaries Industry Sectors

	Jul 4	Day's chge%	Jul 3	Jul 2	Jul1	Year ago	Div. yld%	Net cover	P/E ratio	Xd adj. ytd	Total Return	1997 High	(date)	1997 Low	(date)	Since Compilation High	(date)	Since Compilation Low	(date)
10 MINERAL EXTRACTION(20)	4660.51	-0.8	4699.79	4608.48	4582.02	3530.00	3.28	2.01	18.96	88.92	2087.89	4699.79	3/7	2891	3/1	4699.79	3/7/97	980.20	19.2.86
12 Extractive Industries(5)	4347.63	-0.3	4362.56	4403.37	4434.94	4203.44	3.62	2.38	14.49	104.80	1328.93	4609.25	13/6	3774.12	5/2	4768.29	7/5/96	1000.00	31/12/85
15 Oil, Integrated(3)	4874.73	-0.8	4914.48	4797.59	4766.89	3612.40	3.42	1.95	18.74	94.47	2245.58	4914.48	3/7	4005.84	3/1	4914.48	3/7/97	982.30	20/2/86
16 Oil Exploration & Prod(12)	3790.79	-1.7	3855.46	3793.63	3733.15	2475.32	1.53	2.21	36.94	39.12	2323.21	3855.46	3/7	3233.63	6/1	3944.10	8/8/90	650.30	28/7/86
20 GEN INDUSTRIALS(265)	1872.67	-1.2	1896.16	1926.33	1922.14	2024.18	4.27	1.90	15.41	42.03	1070.21	2071.14	11/3	1872.67	4/7	2232.68	2/2/94	986.10	14/1/86
21 Building & Construction(35)	1374.75	-0.6	1383.03	1359.71	1351.81	1193.33	3.23	1.96	19.77	26.30	1196.89	1194.01	13/6	1194.01	2/1	2125.60	16/7/87	538.30	9/9/92
22 Building Matls & Merchs(30)	1798.38	-1.3	1821.22	1860.49	1858.57	1899.45	4.49	2.82	9.87	41.69	950.40	1950.15	13/6	1787.73	10/1	2393.22	24/1/94	954.80	9/9/92
23 Chemicals(26)	2351.34	-1.0	2375.40	2438.95	2428.76	2422.62	4.50	1.48	18.83	64.32	1173.17	2512.70	13/6	2223.68	28/4	2609.64	24/4/96	979.50	14/1/86
24 Diversified Industries(15)	1288.54	-1.6	1309.60	1358.98	1339.56	1553.54	5.69	1.98	11.10	37.73	764.10	1596.75	11/3	1274.19	10/6	2231.57	2/2/94	964.80	21/1/86
25 Electronic & Elect Equip(37)	2097.44	-1.3	2124.22	2047.60	2045.50	2301.75	3.78	1.62	20.40	18.04	1123.40	2386.20	14/1	1985.79	5/6	2480.07	3/6/96	986.80	29/9/86
26 Engineering(68)	2431.06	-0.8	2449.96	2517.49	2525.55	2456.74	3.53	2.27	15.58	50.97	1534.22	2664.84	6/1	2431.06	4/7	2678.41	21/10/96	962.80	10/11/87
27 Engineering, Vehicles(13)	2674.73	-3.2	2764.32	2845.48	2846.86	3008.47	3.84	†	+	56.04	1440.71	3075.29	9/1	2674.73	4/7	3313.39	29/11/96	995.60	14/1/86
28 Paper, Pckg & Printing(27)	1967.73	-1.1	1989.83	2018.87	2007.76	2581.22	5.34	1.88	12.48	58.15	860.14	2597.20	12/3	1967.73	4/7	3142.02	11/7/95	973.30	14/1/86
29 Textiles & Apparel(14)	1005.65	-2.6	1032.67	1040.29	1060.49	1369.28	6.96	0.99	18.22	42.55	662.38	1106.16	17/1	1005.65	4/7	2325.00	2/10/87	960.60	24/9/90
80 INVESTMENT TRUSTS(127)	3445.11		3444.42	3434.19	3418.57	3126.97	2.20	1.17	48.78	45.69	1237.09	3487.87	13/6	3095.53	2/1	3487.87	13/6/97	977.20	14/1/86
89 FTSE All-Share(910)	2260.61	-0.4	2269.36	2240.42	2230.43	1868.75	3.43	1.94	18.76	43.95	2002.25	2269.36	3/7	1989.78	2/1	2269.36	3/7/97	61.92	13/12/74
105 FSE All-Share ex IT(783)	2260.68	-0.4	2269.73	2240.06	2230.08	-	3.47	1.96	18.39	12.60	1029.67	2269.73	3/7	1085.67	9/5	2269.73	3/7/97	1085.67	9/5/97
FTSE Fledging	1257.62	+0.1	1255.75	1253.25	1251.73	1247.82	3.20	0.81	48.19	22.85	1361.66	1347.52	13/3	1223.48	2/1	1778.30	2/2/94	31.14	12/12/94
FTSE Fledging ex IT	1259.16	+0.1	1257.29	1254.38	1253.90	1260.70	3.56	0.79	44.56	22.89	1342.03	1368.01	13/3	1244.06	2/1	1778.30	2/2/94	26.13	12/12/94
FTSE AIM	1056.1	+0.1	1054.5	1053.6	1051.0	-	1.04	1.188	0.00†	3.69	967.41	1212.2	9/5	1051.0	1/7	1212.2	9/5/97	1051.0	1/7/97

always be influenced in their choice by the Standard and Poor credit rating of a company. This particular influence is very important because when the London market is enjoying a 'bull' phase, demand for the better-quality British shares is spread all over the world. In times of a bear market, these investments are likely to attract a greater volume of selling orders because the overseas holders will probably take fright and start dumping their holdings.

Figure 9.3 is the chart of the movement of the FTSE 100, the Dow Jones Industrial 30 share index and the smaller companies index over the period 1 January to 12 June 1997. It demonstrates my point very well indeed. You will see how closely the two major indices have followed each other upwards, and how the smaller capitalised companies have shown hardly any growth over the same period.

In fact, by far the greatest volume of trading during this period took place in the financial sector which consists of the clearing banks such as Lloyds TSB, National Westminster, Barclays, HSBC/Midland as well as the building societies which have come to the market and changed their status into banks. The graph in Figure 9.3 underlines my point about the need for researching the market activities, because if you were to look at the FTSE 100 index only, at first sight it would appear that the share prices of all the leading companies in the market were rising steadily: not only following a rising trend from the beginning of April, but beginning to resemble a rocket launch since the beginning of June.

I have been in the market too long to be carried away by the euphoria which this sort of performance tends to generate among investors generally. Usually such meteoric rises tend to be matched by similar falls in share prices, for one reason or another. I have explained 'fair values' as well as the fact that the market over reacts *in both directions* and that its natural tendency is to return to the moving average even though the trend line may be following an upward path. Consequently, this chart not only represents an overbought situation more clearly than words can describe one, but if you dig out the driving factor which, as I have said, is the financial sector, you will find confirmation if you apply both fundamental and technical analysis to those shares.

Fig 9.3 FTSE, Dow Jones Industrial 30-share Index, smaller companies index 1 January to 12 June 1997

(Source: *Financial Times*)

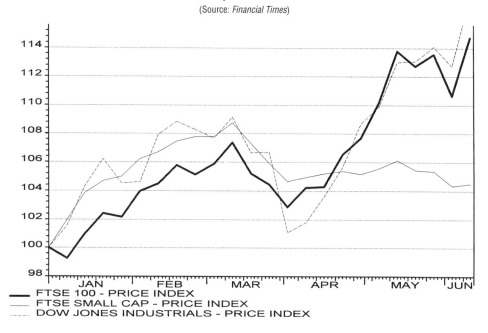

FTSE 100 - PRICE INDEX
FTSE SMALL CAP - PRICE INDEX
DOW JONES INDUSTRIALS - PRICE INDEX

Under such circumstances, the investor should *not* rush out to buy shares in the banks or building societies until they have fallen back to a more reasonable level. This is not to say that they should not be held in a portfolio – they certainly should, and if you hold them already you should stay with them for the ride. But if they are over-priced when they turn downwards, then, after such an abnormal rise in such a short time (refer back to the section on Short-term indicators in Chapter 5), you should consider selling them to lock in your profits and buy them back at a lower price. This example and advice applies to any sector or individual share where the behaviour follows a similar pattern. It is unlikely to occur very often, but when it does, taking profits should be the first and most important consideration of any portfolio manager worth his salt. After all, managing your own portfolio successfully is what this book is all about.

Nevertheless, because of the huge number of shares in issue for these companies coupled with the fact that all the big institutional fund managers and pension funds will be unwilling to sell even if the market takes a downturn, there is likely to be less of a drop in the share price of these companies compared with those of the smaller ones. In addition, the number of market makers who are dealing in these shares is much greater than is the case for the smaller ones and so this fact provides a buttress for the share price because the market makers are unlikely to be stuffed with selling orders without the ability to pass on some unwanted stock either to another market maker or to an institutional or private buyer. The reason for any major fall in the price of a leader in its sector is much more likely to be as a result of some fundamental bad news in the market place.

For the long-term investor, the trend in a share price and, of course that of the market as a whole is of much more significance than short-term fluctuations in the share price. Therefore, it is obvious that the bigger companies whose shares are being traded frequently and in large volumes are the ones which are likely to rise at a faster rate than the rest of the market overall provided that the market trend in general is upwards and these investments will give you more safety in the long run and thus a better chance of beating the RPI index. So the next question which must arise is how to find the shares which are the shares which are highly priced and seem to be set to go on going up, and look for the reasons why the market opinion appears to favour this view.

We have already seen that one of the main reasons for the price of a share going up and remaining high is because of the support which it receives from sustained demand from investors. I realise that this is an oversimplification, but there is some truth in the answer to the question 'why is the price rising?': 'because there are more buyers than sellers'.

The fundamental reason why people buy one share rather than another is because they expect the price to rise, and this expectation is predicated upon an anticipated rise in earnings. That is to say that they expect the company to continue to make greater profits next year and continue to maintain the increase in the years to come. In other words, the expectation is for fundamental growth

> 'For the long-term investor, the trend in a share price and, of course that of the market as a whole is of much more significance than short-term fluctuations in the share price.'

167

within the company. If the market has faith in the management of the company, because not only has it demonstrated its ability to increase profits in the past but also its published plans for future growth make sense to the investor, then the market will continue to support the share price.

When is a share expensive and when is it cheap to buy?

This is a question which I am often asked and there are two methods which you can use to answer it.

- The first is to establish the trading range of the share over the last few months and the way to do this has been described in some detail in the first part of this book.
- The second is to estimate what can be described as a 'fair value' for the share based on a combination of asset value and current earnings. The way in which this is calculated is fairly arbitrary and for simplicity I take the average share price over the last two years as a starting point. Most shares are standing at a price which is above or below this arbitrary valuation.

■ **EXAMPLE: Allied Domecq**

Let us take an example of how this fair value figure can vary over a period of years and try to learn some lessons from it. I have chosen the history over the last three years of Allied Domecq, previously named Allied Lyons.

Three or four years ago, the group consisted of a chain of breweries (Allied) and a number of companies whose business was the manufacture, distribution and retailing of certain foods (Lyons). The brewing side owned breweries in Scotland, Burton-on-Trent, Birmingham, Leeds and London, and made 'Babycham' in Bristol. Lyons manufactured ice cream, Lyonsmaid foods; and there were other smaller similar enterprises as well as a large catering service company: a diversified group. Such a mini conglomerate requires very high levels of management expertise from board level downwards including manufacturing and distribution skills as well as marketing ability in two very competitive industries.

The beer was sold through supermarket chains and off-licences as well as public houses, most of which were 'tied' to the brewery. That is to say that the tenants or managers had to buy their beer and spirits from the brewery, they were not free to obtain supplies from any other source even if they could have done so more cheaply. EEC rules were brought in to restrict the breweries to no more than 2,000 licensed public houses tied to any one brewer. Allied owned over 4,000.

The restrictions placed on the ownership of tied pubs made me look at the brewing sector as a whole since they would affect all brewers. I talked to the various brewing analysts to find out what plans the industry might have to combat such a threat to their earnings potential. It became obvious that the big brewers would have to diversify into other activities to maintain their earnings and most of the rest were looking at the leisure industry in the UK in one form or another. Allied chose to divest itself of all its food interests and concentrate on growing bigger through international acquisitions in the wine and spirits trade.

At that time, the fair value of the share was about 380p, before they started to try to sell off the Lyons businesses.

There followed a fairly disastrous chain of events. First they sold the individual food companies at a time when interest rates were high thereby getting less for each one than they should have done. Second, they sold the Showerings Babycham business at a ridiculously low price, even though it was a drinks business, because competition was hotting up in the peripheral drinks business outside the core wines and spirits trade. Third they entered into an agreement with Carlsberg to merge the Tetley brewery in Leeds to try to build their market share in the lager market. The agreement was very restrictive as far as the Allied shareholders were concerned, and the board has been trying to dispose of the Allied holding ever since without success.

Morale among the middle and lower management in the brewing side was bad and getting steadily worse as redundancies were increasing. In order to comply with EEC regulations concerning the number of tied pubs, the board decided to reduce the number of tenants and replace them with managers in as many of the pubs that they could among those which they wished to keep. There is never the same incentive for a manager, compared with a tenant, to put in the extra hours to make the premises more attractive or to devise new ways of increasing the profitability of the premises.

However, at the same time that all this reconstruction was going on, a rumour started to go round the market that a very rich Hong Kong Chinese family who had a business in Canada might be about to make a bid for the company. The shares reached a level of over 700p for a time, and when the anticipated bid failed to emerge, they dropped back to around 550p. I felt that the fair value for the share was about 475p. The following year the bid rumour was revived, and the share price rose again to the 700p mark for a time and then fell back again.

The buyers consisted of those who genuinely thought that the company had sorted out its problems arising from being a diversified company and was now set to increase its profits steadily over the years, and those who were seeking to make a short-term profit as a result of the bid becoming a reality.

During this period, the board decided to spend the money it had obtained from the various disposals it had made in the Lyons food businesses to buy the business of Domecq. This company, which was largely family owned, had been established for a very long time and its principal products were sherry, wine and brandy. It had a number of very strong brands well-known in its markets, which included Spain and South America principally. Some years previously, Allied had acquired the business of Hiram Walker in the USA, a well-established distributor of wines and spirits throughout the North American continent and owner of some of the leading brand names in US-produced whiskeys and gin. On the face of it, the expansion plans seemed to be well-thought-out and a firm grip appeared to have been established on the major markets in the Western world. The company changed its name to Allied Domecq.

I raised my fair value figure to 550p. When such a takeover occurs, where there is a substantial shareholding belonging to one person or family, it is common practice to restrict them from selling their shares in the enlarged group for a period after the 'marriage' so that the market in the shares is maintained in an orderly fashion. It became known that immediately after the restricted period had ended, the Domecq family had sold their entire holding in Allied Domecq – which did not say much for their faith in the future of the company. It may have been that they thought that they got a very good deal in the first place which went beyond their expectations, or perhaps they could see the problems confronting the wine and spirits trade more clearly than was apparent to the board of Allied Domecq. Nevertheless, such actions never bode well for the ordinary shareholder or private investor.

I lowered my fair value to 450p. Subsequently, the company made a further act of bad judgement when it incurred losses of several millions of pounds through hedging US dollar earnings against a future £/$US exchange rate and got the anticipated movement the wrong way. The finance director left, and a few months later there was a change of chairman. I lowered my fair value to 380p.

Now during this whole period, it was perfectly possible to make good profits for my clients, and indeed I did so, but the share changed from being one which had been regarded for many years previously as a well-run, good solid blue-chip, to one where the management seemed to have lost all sense of direction and lacked any real ideas for growth, let alone survival, in an industry which was undergoing fundamental changes.

Over the same period, the other major brewers diversified into the leisure industry and they did this in a variety of ways. Bass, Worthington and Scottish and Newcastle built theme parks and placed a great emphasis on changing their pubs so that they became places where the whole family could go for something to eat as well as drink. A lot of money was spent on changing the image of the public house to one where it became a place of entertainment for the whole family rather than simply a male preserve devoted to the sale and consumption of booze. The advertising budget was increased and large sums of money were spent to try to maintain, or increase market share. Their success can be judged from the steady growth in their share prices over the period.

So what lessons can be learned from this saga?

Fair value

It is very important to keep the assessment of a fair value in the back of your mind, particularly when it comes to buying a share, as well as during the period in which you hold it in your portfolio. The market always over reacts to any news especially when it comes to rumours of a bid or merger, and it is very easy to get carried away with the euphoria generated as a by-product of the concentration of Press comment and small investor buying which will often push the price up to unsustainable levels. You can always check with your stockbroker to see whether there have been frequent large purchases of the share which will tell you if the bigger funds are supporting the share. However, even so the assessment of fair value remains with you and the best way to arrive at this figure is to use commonsense.

Market sentiment

Market sentiment must *not* be confused with market enthusiasm, particularly when there is a bid or merger rumour in the air. The latter is caused by sudden and widespread interest from outside the market and is likely to die just as fast as it was born. Market sentiment is generated by an analytical (and often cynical) opinion about the ability of the management to keep on delivering the goodies. It can take a long time to generate respect and supportive market sentiment, but it can be blown away in moments if expectations are not met. If anything happens which is unexpected, such as a sudden and unforeseen profits warning, market sentiment can easily turn from amity to hostility. You can sense the atmosphere generally from the responsible Press comments.

HOW TO ASSESS A COMPANY LOCALLY

Obviously there are many companies whose products are impossible to assess locally. Guided missile or nuclear submarine manufacturers to name but two. However, there are many that you can whose products are retailed in every high street. You can get a very good 'feel' about the popularity of the product or the enthusiasm (or lack of it) for the company behind the product or service by talking to those people whose job it is to retail the goods. Everyone has to buy food and so you can do your own market research by looking at the popularity of one supermarket chain store compared with another. You can do the same thing with DIY stores, chemists, petrol stations (look at the prices), clothes stores, etc. ... Do not be afraid to ask questions, because the management always likes to talk about their business. They are unlikely to tell you that they are suffering from falling sales, but your own observations about their prices compared with those of their competitors and the attitude of the staff to service and general appearance and efficiency will tell you a lot, particularly if you record your impressions over a period of time.

CHANGE OF SENIOR MANAGEMENT

Whenever there is a change of chairman, or a substantial change in the members of the board of directors, you should immediately put yourself on alert if you hold the share in your portfolio. The historic progress of the company's profits and its general development will have been made under the guidance of the chairman. If this has been satisfactory so far, it will probably have been achieved because the chairman has a strong personality and has had a clear idea of strategic planning and managed to get executives in place who are totally committed to his or her aims and objectives. Furthermore, the executives will almost certainly have enjoyed the trust and support of the chairman and been left alone to carry out his or her plans for achieving the targets for growth and expansion.

A new person at the helm faces a number of tests, both from the rest of the board within the company and from the observers in the market outside. At best, they will take time to make up their minds about the ability of the new captain and the market will only form an opinion when the financial results are published emanating from the regime under the new management. One thing is certain, and that is that if you do not hold the shares already but had been contemplating buying some, *wait and see*. There are exceptions to this rule, obviously, such as a situation where the previous crew have managed the business so badly that they have run the share price into the ground and a new management is much more likely to make a success of the company than the last lot. However, under such circumstances, the share will have ceased to be a safe investment and become a speculative punt much more suited to trading in the short-term. The new management will have to take quite a long time to gain market approval.

Never forget that companies are run by people, not machines. People are fallible and their mistakes in judgement can easily damage your capital.

MERGERS

Another aspect to be considered when looking at a share to buy is whether the published expansion plans are likely to fall foul of the

Monopolies and Mergers Committee (MMC). Because if they are, then you are unlikely to see the sort of growth in earnings which the chairman is anticipating achieving until the MMC has cleared the proposed acquisition, and this can take months.

At the time of writing this book, the merger between Guinness and Grand Metropolitan has just been announced. I reprint an article, with kind permission from the City Editor of the *Sunday Telegraph*, which comments on the plan and which underlines the point about management made above (see Figure 9.4).

It is interesting to note that at the time when the plan was announced by the London Stock Exchange, the price of Allied Domecq rose. This was simply because the speculative reaction in the market was to wonder immediately if Allied might be the next target to attract a suitor, and not because of any intrinsic enhancement of the underlying asset value or earnings potential in the company. As I have said before, there is a widely held misconception that the City is a place where there is a whole stack of information which is denied to the ordinary investor living out in the country and away from the hot-house of the Square Mile. This is simply not true, although there are indeed always going to be some small groups of people who are involved in discussions having to do with possible mergers or acquisitions, but the rules under the SFA are so strict that if any of that information were to be used for personal gain or indeed for the benefit of their clients, then it is an offence for which you can go to prison. So the point that I am really making is that what is available to those in the country or away from the City is no more and no less than that which is available to those who work in the market. I reproduce another article from the *Sunday Telegraph* concerning this Guinness/Grand Met merger because it demonstrates a number of points which are germane to any decision as to whether to buy or not (see Figure 9.5).

The first point is that the proposed merger brings together, as the article says, two of the top premier branded consumer goods companies in Britain. If this merger were to go ahead there would obviously be a great deal of duplication in terms of people who are the most expensive item in any company's costs. Teams of salesmen, adminis-

Fig 9.4

(Source: *Sunday Telegraph*)

How I uncorked a £22bn merger

Last summer, when I revealed that Guinness was planning a hostile bid for Grand Metropolitan, I never expected the two businesses would actually come together. The documents were very detailed and Guinness had clearly spent millions on preparing the bid. But the financial effects looked too strained for such a deal to work and Guinness had had to make some heroic assumptions about the value of Grand Met's business for a break up to recoup the cost of the offer.

But my story had a whole number of effects that I hadn't fully appreciated until this week. For a start, everyone in the City said it seemed a good idea to put the spirits businesses of the two companies together. At last, Guinness and Grand Met could talk about the benefits, using my story as a pretext.

The smart man in the affair was John McGrath, Grand Met's chief executive. He knew that he had to get Grand Met's share price up at all costs. If it had continued to slide, as Allied Domecq's has, a break-up bid would have become a real possibility.

Since last summer he has breathed new life into Grand Met's shares by telling the City everything it wanted to hear. He promised no more nasty sur-prises, to reduce the debt and, most importantly, to improve the returns in the business. Without this Guinness deal last week he would have announced a share buy-back to curry even more favour.

Grand Met's shares rose and trans-formed it from possible victim to poten-tial partner. McGrath's prize is a rich one; not only does Grand Met take the major-ity of the new business but McGrath himself also becomes group chief execu-tive. If Grand Met had fallen prey to Guinness, he would have been out on his ear.

I still have worries about the deal, though. The competition issue seems straightforward. Sooner or later GMG Brands will sell a few products, such as J&B Rare, to assuage the authorities, which should do the trick.

No, my main worry is management. Tony Greener has always struck me as a man who finds it so difficult to delegate that he probably cuts his own hair. At one stage he was Guinness's chairman, chief executive and head of the spirits division. How will he cope with playing second fiddle to McGrath as chief executive? The last thing this new corporate jugger-naut needs is a struggle over the steering wheel.

tration departments, transport and distribution methods can all be combined with the probability of considerable reductions in the number of staff required, with consequent reduction in wages costs.

In addition to that, there would be probably be a substantial reduc-tion in the spend on advertising because both firms will have been using different agencies and devoting large sums of money to each one, used to fight each other as well as other competitors.

Fig 9.5

(Source: *Sunday Telegraph*)

SPIRIT MIXERS

When The Sunday Telegraph revealed a planned Guinness takeover of Grand Met last year, both sides ruled it out. Now they are coming together in a £22bn merger. **Richard Newton** examines why they have changed their minds and the rationale behind the new giant

At the end of a lonely track on the Isle of Skye sits the Talisker malt whisky distillery. Should you turn up unannounced, it seems deserted. There is not, after all, a lot to do while you wait for scotch to age the requisite 10, 12 or even 16 years. At least the lights from the distillery help guide climbers on the nearby Black Cuillin mountain range.

Standing on the windswept hillside, it is impossible to believe that Talisker is an outpost of a £22bn conglomerate. But that is what it became part of last week when Guinness and Grand Metropolitan announced their plans for a merger to create a business to be called GMG Brands.

Compare the age-old tradition of the Guinness-owned distillery with Grand Met's frantic Burger King restaurant on the corner of Leicester Square and you begin to have an idea of the immensity of the project that the two companies have undertaken.

The merger brings together two of the top premier UK branded consumer goods companies, each complete with legions of marketing and sales executives steeped in strong and separate corporate cultures. Guinness, quoted on the London Stock Exchange since 1886, is not only famous for producing the stout but is also the world's predominant whisky company.

Grand Met's International Distillers & Vintners division is in its own right the largest spirits company in the world and after a period of empire building under Allen (now Lord) Sheppard, its former chairman, in the 1980s it now owns some of the most famous food brands in the world, notably Burger King, Pillsbury and Green Giant.

But this merger is about spirits. This is where the two companies make the huge part of their profits and it is the problems facing the spirits industry that have forced them to merge.

Guinness, whose brands include Johnnie Walker and Gordon's Gin, and Grand Met, whose portfolio lists J&B Rare and Smirnoff Vodka, generate huge sums of cash. But spirits consumption in the developed world is flat or slowly declining, and even the strongest marketing seems unable to turn that around.

The announcement at 7.30 am last Monday that these two giants were merging shook the drinks industry. Grand Met's communications team was besieged by calls from within the company as well as outside. "Staff rang up stunned and said they had leaped out of the bath and others had fallen off their exercise bikes. People were amazed," said the head of corporate affairs. Once the news had sunk in, however, people began to understand it.

According to George Bull, Grand Met's chairman: "Everybody realised that sooner or later there had to be a consolidation in the industry, a coalescence. we had been looking at all the alternatives, and putting Guinness and Grand Met together was one of them. But we had books on others and others had books on us and others I'm sure had books on others. But it was obvious that we

two fit together well, like a hand and glove."

Last year *The Sunday Telegraph* revealed that Guinness was working on secret plans for the take over of Grand Met, called Project Reflection. It would have entailed a hostile bid, and, if successful, would have been followed by the disposal of all Grand Met's food operations and Burger King. In the aftermath of the news, Guinness denied that it would bid, but clearly the idea did not go away.

The drinks portfolios of the two companies are almost perfect matches. Guinness's product muscle in whisky and geographic strength in developing markets, for example, is complemented by Grand Met's product strengths in tequila and vodka and geographic power base in the US.

'Everybody realised that there had to be a consolidation in the industry. It was obvious that Guinness and Grand Met fit together well, like a hand and glove'

But according to Philip Yea, the finance director of Guinness and soon to be group finance director of the merged group: "The strategic case was just as brilliant last year as it was this year. But this year we could justify the deal."

The problem was that a hostile takeover would involve a massive takeover premium. As Bull said: "The question of bidding and paying a premium price had become so enormous that, combined with the relatively slow growth performance of the spirits business in the world at large, the likelihood of a payback on such an acquisition had become impossible."

But for a no-premium deal to succeed both the industry and the City had to accept that agreed mergers were the only way forward. According to Yea: "The leak to *The Sunday Telegraph* last year demonstrated that if a premium was involved it involved destruction of value. That story allowed the stockmarket to talk openly about these issues. I was in a meeting the next Monday and we talked about industry consolidation in a way that we hadn't done before."

In April, less than a year later at one of their regular pow-wows over dinner Bull "popped the question" to Tony Greener, his opposite number at Guinness.

While Greener says he didn't expect the deal to be suggested "in that way", the timing was right. "You cannot do a no-premium merger unless the price is right." In the past six months the value of both companies has moved into line, making a merger of equals possible.

After the dinner at Dukes Hotel Greener summoned Yea and he began to work through the numbers whilst Greener went on a planned business trip to Africa.

According to Yea: "You cannot have the chairman

cancelling his engagements because then people will say 'Ah ha'. That's one of the stresses of a deal like this; you still have to do the day job, but you have a night job, too."

John McGrath, the chief executive of Grand Met and the pending chief executive of GMG, said it was critical that nothing should leak out. "History shows that when mergers are in the public domain the track record of getting them through to completion is very, very poor. We only told people about the deal on a need-to-know basis."

Guinness's in-house lawyer, who was already planning a two-week holiday, was roped in to help. "As far as the internal Guinness world was concerned he was away. But we had set up an offsite base at the Churchill Hotel and he worked from there", said Yea.

The tiny team working on Project Bath, as it became codenamed, only really started to charge ahead, on April 28, the day after the board members of the two companies – Grand Met (code-named Garden) and Guinness (Bristol) – agreed to pursue the deal.

Greener said: "The most remarkable thing was that this team of four people – Bull, McGrath, Yea and myself – plus our advisers were able to put this thing together in only 10 days. The urgency was to keep the press out."

Last weekend a team of about 60, was summoned to the Gray's Inn Road office of SJ Berwin, Grand Met's lawyers. It included SBC Warburg, Grand Met's investment bankers, and Guinness advisers Lazards and Norton Rose.

While the announcement on Monday stunned the companies' staff and the City, it confirmed the worst nightmares of the other large drinks companies, Allied Domecq and Seagram which will be dwarfed by the monolithic GMG.

Sir Christopher Hogg, Allied's chairman, assigned a task force to examine the implications and warned of the possible threat to competition. Bob Matschullat, chief financial officer at Seagram, didn't need to. He immediately denounced it as anti-competitive. "I don't know whether they think the regulators are asleep." he complained.

But both Seagram and Allied know the deal will probably sail through the EC which has been ceded the regulatory role by the UK authorities and that the US regulators will probably pass it in return for the sacrifice of some brands or distribution rights. the best they can hope for is to pick up some of the brands which are ditched by GMG to keep regulators happy or because they overlap.

Analysts and industry insiders think that GMG Brands may have to sacrifice J&B Rare, Grand Met's top selling whisky, which is hugely popular in the US and Spain but outsold by the world number one, Guinness's Johnnie Walker. It is also the only major brand where there is clear overlap and the competitors would love to buy it.

McGrath dismissed the Seagram outcry as "predictable". He said: "If you are a regulator looking at our business you have to look at alcohol in total. People do not drink just scotch or just gin or just beer. People take a broader view and I'm sure the authorities will too."

In terms of world spirits consumption, the merged group would have a 5 per cent market share and under the narrower definition of western style spirits, which are the only sort that GMG is interested in producing, it has less than 10 per cent.

The other problem being faced by GMG is the rebel in their midst – Bernard Arnault, chairman of LVMH, the French luxury goods company which owns 14 per cent of Guinness.

Arnault has been sharply critical of the company's performance in the past. His statement objecting to the merger and proposing that the Guinness, Grand Met and LVMH should merge and break off the brewing and food businesses to create a pure drinks company constituted a clear invitation to third parties to disrupt the party.

But Bull is philosophical: "There is always the outside chance that someone may want to see if they can find an angle. But we cannot see a better angle."

In the near future, once GMG has realised its £175m a year cost savings, it will be throwing off huge sums of cash. "Between us we are generating £900m of cash," said Greener.

By giving 60p a share to shareholders at a cost of £2.4bn, they can maintain interest cover at just below six times. It also gives the impression that even in an agreed takeover the City still demands that the shareholders receive a cash payment.

But after a couple of years the interest cover will start to rise again. "We won't be making massive value-destroying acquisitions", said Greener. "We are absolutely committed to generating shareholder value."

The challenge for GMG Brands is to ensure that it does not recreate the same problems of how to achieve growth in a dull drinks market. The real job is to persuade us to raise a glass of Talisker more regularly.

Now in any such proposal, the objective is to enhance the value of the underlying shares, and if it can be shown that there will be considerable cost savings as a result of the merger then there is an apparent justification for paying a price which is higher than the current market value of the share in question. Such payment can be made in several forms. For example, if one company makes a bid for another at a price which is above the current market price, the amount in excess of current market price (called a premium) has to be justified to the shareholders of the bidding company and future cost savings which are likely to result in higher overall earnings of the enlarged group is one obvious way. However, the proposition here is a merger, so there is no battle to be fought. Nevertheless the shareholders of both companies have to be convinced that they will benefit from the union, because the values of both companies are more or less equal. This merger can be described as 'a no premium' deal.

Now, when a merger or takeover is proposed, whether the companies are large or small, there will be shareholders in each case who will argue that their company would do better in the future if left alone to continue to plough its own furrow. When the companies concerned are large blue-chip enterprises, whose shares form part of the core holdings of major institutions such as insurance companies and pension funds as well as many other portfolios, there is bound to be considerable dissent. However, the reason why the Guinness/Grand Met merger is probably more likely to be accepted with minimal fuss lies in the consensus view concerning the future and difficulties of the drink trade. In other words, market opinion, so vital to the maintenance of support for share prices, as I have repeatedly stressed in this book, is almost certainly to view this merger beneficialy and give it a blessing.

One interesting point to consider is that there might be a concentration of effort on the drink side of the business compared with the food side. This would indicate that the merger is for defensive reasons to try to use cost savings as a tool for enhancement of earnings rather than because one set of management thinks it can make the other company expand organically in the market for its goods. If this is the case, then the share price of the enlarged group will not necessarily continue to grow because there is a limit to the amount of costs which can be saved. Look what has happened to Allied Domecq! Such success or otherwise as might be forthcoming in the future will show up quite easily by monitoring the ROCE.

READING THE PRESS

I find that very often it is the smaller pieces which appear in the Press which alert me to interesting situations. It does not require a full-blown article to attract my attention, and two examples of just such comment are shown in Figures 9.6 and 9.7, one concerning a company called Medeva, from Market Miscellany, the *Sunday Telegraph*, and the other about Tesco, also from the *Sunday Telegraph*, which provides exactly the kind of lead to which I am referring.

Fig 9.6
(Source: *Sunday Telegraph*)

Medeva standing on a big discount

SHARES in Medeva have slumped, following news of weak sales of Ionamin, its anti-obesity drug. On Friday they closed at 274p, down 17 per cent from a 12-month high of 330p in March. A number of positive analysts' notes are in circulation which anticipate that trading in the rest of the business under the direction of Bill Bogie, chief executive, is performing strongly. Moreover City watchers, including UBS analyst David Grogan, think that the concerns over the poor trading in Ionamin are overdone. Even though forecasts for Ionamin's 1997 sales have been cut by about a quarter, the effect on earnings per share should be a reduction of no more than 3 per cent. On this basis Medeva, which UBS expects to make profits of £120m this year and £132m next, is on a 1998 price earnings ratio of 11 compared to an industry average of about 17. The heavy discount presents a significant buying opportunity.

Fig 9.7
(Source: *Sunday Telegraph*)

Tesco cheaper

SAINSBURY'S remains at least 4 per cent more expensive to shop at than Tesco, according to research carried out by Taylor Nelson AGB. The figures show that although the chain has kept prices low at key shopping periods and has boosted points on its reward card, the cost of a wide range of products has steadily inched up throughout 1997.

The history and growth of Medeva resembles that of Glaxo Wellcome in its early days, which is not surprising because its recent expansion was engineered by the same man who built up Glaxo. Here is a very good example of my earlier statement that companies are run by people, not machines, and you are backing people who have proved themselves to be successful in their particular field.

The quality newspapers and the financial journals and newsletters are a profitable source of information and tips for making money. They are available to everyone and all it requires to get the best out of them is to spend a little bit of time reading them regularly. If you do not do your own research and consequently miss opportunities, you have only yourself to blame.

SUMMARY

In this chapter, we have demonstrated how to:

- establish fair value for a share by using commonsense and constantly questioning the current price so that *you* arrive at a fair value using fundamental analysis;
- establish whether a share is expensive or cheap using the trading range as a guide coupled with the trend over the last twelve months;
- find out what is the current market sentiment for a given share by talking to your broker;
- do your own local market research by talking to purveyors of goods and services and your own powers of observation;
- be alerted if there is a sudden change of senior management in a company in which you hold shares, or may be about to buy some.

THE KEY INDICATORS

INTRODUCTION

In this chapter we examine in detail the six key indicators to which we referred in the first part of the book. They are:

- earnings per share (EPS)
- profit (loss) before tax
- trading profit (loss)
- shareholders' funds
- dividend cover
- return on capital employed (ROCE).

As I have said before, the average private investor is faced with a mass of data both in the Press and in the company *Report and Accounts* which can be very daunting. Most people think that you have to be an accountant to interpret what is contained in these documents, but this is just not so.

In fact, with a little practice, you can extract the information for the key indicators in a few minutes, and the picture you get will tell you a great deal about the company's progress, its financial strength, its management and the safety or otherwise of shareholders' funds. Unless the picture that emerges from analysing the key indicators is one with which you are happy, you should not buy the share, or, if you hold it already, you should think seriously about selling it.

These indicators are very easy to find, and with only one exception, they do not require any mathematical computation on your part. All you have to do is to recognise an obvious trend and apply the rules described in this chapter.

The key indicators can be found in the company *Report and Accounts*, but they only go back two years and the indicators are not calculated for you. The place to get the data from is the company Extel card which your stockbroker will supply if you ask for it, and an example is shown in Figure 10.1.

'All you have to do is to recognise an obvious trend and apply the rules described in this chapter.'

Figure 10.1 shows the Extel card for J Sainsbury PLC, and the six key indicators are marked to show you where to look. They all follow a similar pattern in their construction, so you should have no difficulty in extracting the indicators for other companies from their cards.

Do not make the mistake of comparing interim results with those for the full accounting period. This is usually a year, but sometimes companies decide to change their accounting period and it might cover a month or two over or under a full year. If they do so, it will be announced on the card.

EARNINGS PER SHARE (EPS)

This indicator, shown as (1) in Figure 10.1, shows the amount of profit which the company has made for the period divided by the number of *ordinary* shares in issue. It is *not* the amount of profit which is distributed by way of dividend. What it tells you is whether or not the company is earning good profits for the ordinary shareholder.

Since any set of accounts merely represents a 'snapshot' of a moment in the life of a company, you can get very little information, if any, from one year's results. So you must look at the trend over a period of at least five years to see whether the management has been able to increase the earnings on your investment, year by year. Quite often you will see a fluctuation in the EPS record, and the first thing to find out is why did it occur.

There could be several reasons. Very often a company has got a subsidiary which has been making losses and in the year in which it is sold or closed down, the losses become considerable. Sometimes companies are more vulnerable than others to abnormally high interest rates and this cost can reduce earnings considerably. Whatever the reason, you need to satisfy yourself as to the cause and decide whether it is an on-going problem or attributable to an event which is unlikely to recur. Essentially, the trend should demonstrate a steady growth over the five-year period, because it is largely upon this factor that market sentiment will depend.

Fig 10.1 Extel card for J Sainsbury, PLC

(Source: Extel Financial Limited)

Company Report	COMPANY RESEARCH	May 7, 1997

SAINSBURY, J PLC

Security Name
ORD GBP0.25

Shares in Issue
1,841,428,324

Latest Dividend

Net	8.8p
Gross	11p
Tax	2.2p
Div Type	Financial dividend carrying optional alternatives
Pay Date	July 25, 1997
Ex Date	May 19, 1997

Country of Quotation
United Kingdom

Industrial Classification (SEC)
Retailers, Food

Closing Price
£3.49 up £0.03 (1%) Cum dividend

Market Capitalisation
£6,426,584,850

P/E Ratio*
15.86

EPS*
N/A

*Last reported 12 month earnings

Gross Dividend Yield
4.41%

Market Codes

SEDOL	0767640
TOPIC	SBRY
VALOREN	403712
CUSIP	N/A
TICKER	SBRY

NOTE: The information above relates to the security which is deemed to be the company's prime line.

REGISTERED OFFICE
Stamford House, Stamford Street, London SE1 9LL Tel: 0171 921 6000 Telex: 264241 Fax: 0171 921 6413

REGISTRARS
The Royal Bank of Scotland PLC, Registrars Department, PO Box 82, Caxton House, Redcliffe Way, Bristol BS99 7NH England Tel: 0117 930 6600 Telex: 445845 Fax: 0117 930 6509

DEPOSITARY RECEIPT AGENTS
Citibank NA, 111 Wall Street, New York, New York U S A Tel: +1 212 657-7322/7527

PRESIDENT
PRESIDENT: Lord Sainsbury of Drury Lane; Sir Robert Sainsbury; Lord Sainsbury of Preston Candover KG

DIRECTORS
CHAIRMAN AND CHIEF EXECUTIVE: D.J. Sainsbury
DEPTUTY CHAIRMAN: R.T. Vyner
CHIEF EXECUTIVE: D. Bremner (Appointed 30-07-96)
FINANCE: Rosemary P. Thorne
EXECUTIVE: J.E. Adshead; I.D. Coull; C.I. Harvey (Retiring 08-04-97); K. McCarten; D.J. Clapham; R.P. Whitbread; R. Cooper; D.B. Adriano
NON EXECUTIVE: Dr J.M. Ashworth; C. Thompson; The Rt Hon Sir Timothy Sainsbury MP; Sir Terence Heiser GCB; Sir David Scholey (Appointed 18-07-96)

SECRETARY
N.F. Matthews

AUDITORS
Coopers & Lybrand

BROKERS
S.G. Warburg Securities Ltd

SOLICITORS
Denton Hall

COMPANY HISTORY
Incorporated on 10-11-1922 as a Private Company; Registered No 185647; made Public on 05-07-1973; Re-registered on 01-03-1982 as a Public Limited Company under the Companies Act 1980. In July 1973 10,000,000 Ordinary shares of 25p were offered for sale at 145p per share.

ACTIVITIES
The principal activity of the Group is the retail distribution of food and home improvement and garden products. At 09-03-96, the number of stores were: Sainsbury's 363; Savacentre 12; Homebase 91 and Shaw's 96. The sales area per square foot was: Sainsbury's 9,767; Savacentre 1,034; Homebase 3,453 and Shaw's 3,137.

SUBSIDIARIES
PRINCIPAL: UNITED KINGDOM: Savacentre Ltd; Homebase Ltd (100%); NewMarket Foods Ltd; J. Sainsbury Developments Ltd; Texas Homecare Ltd
USA: Shaw's Supermarkets, Inc
JERSEY: J. Sainsbury (Channel Islands) Ltd

SAINSBURY, J PLC

ASSOCIATED COMPANIES

Breckland Farms Ltd (50%, Pig farming); Giant Food Inc (50% of voting stock and 16.6% of non-voting, USA, Food retailing); Hampden Group PLC (29.9%, DIY Retailing)

CAPITAL at 09-03-96

	AUTHORISED	ISSUED	SHARES ISSUED
Ordinary shares of 25p	£500,000,000	£457,916,901	1,831,667,605

CAPITAL HISTORY

1985/86		2,740,834 Ord	Options
		1,571,405 Ord	Profit Sharing
1986	Sep	2,359,806 Ord	Consideration for further interest in Shaw's Supermarkets, Inc
1986/87		7,708,017 Ord	Options
		1,833,753	Profit Sharing
1987	Jun	20,178,259 Ord	Consideration for further interest in Shaw's Supermarkets, Inc
	Jul	733,866,991 Ord	Scrip – 1:1 (xc-03-07-87)
	Jul	16,509,800 Ord	Consideration for further interest in Shaw's Supermarkets, Inc
1987/88		5,650,737 Ord	Options
		4,427,500 Ord	Profit Sharing
1988/89		3,692,987 Ord	Options
		5,017,936 Ord	Profit Sharing
1989/90		7,641,953 Ord	Options
		4,634,075 Ord	Profit Sharing
1990/91		7,970,550 Ord	Options
		4,632,000 Ord	Profit Sharing
1991	Mar	1,026,715 Ord	Conversion of £2,690,000 5% Capital Bonds
	Apr	56,225,110 Ord	Conversion of £147,300,000 5% Capital Bonds
	Jul	158,733,293 Ord	Rights issue – 1:10 at 312p; cum price 356p; (xr 05-07-91)
	Jul	566,473 Ord	Scrip options (xc 20-05-92)
	Aug	4,477,500 Ord	Profit Sharing
1991/92		7,170,581 Ord	Options
1992	Jan	2,243,186 Ord	Scrip options (xc 11-11-91)
1992/93		3,569,700 Ord	Profit Sharing
		7,812,523 Ord	Options
1992	Jul	4,056,760 Ord	Scrip options (xc 01-06-92)
1993	Jan	1,721,195 Ord	Scrip options (xc 16-11-92)
1993/94		4,160,000 Ord	Profit Sharing
		5,110,227 Ord	Options
1993	Jul		Scrip options (xc 24-05-93)
1994	Jan		Scrip options (xc 29-11-93)
1994/95		4,100,000 Ord	Profit Sharing
		5,672,676 Ord	Options
1995	Jun	4,552,646 Ord	Scrip options (xc 06-06-94)
	Nov	1,719,299 Ord	Scrip options (xc 14-11-94)
		1,350,723 Ord	Profit Sharing
		8,882,619 Ord	Options
1996	Jun	1,915,093 Ord	Scrip options (xc 22-05-96)
		13,069,690 Ord	Conversion of Capital Bond

ACQUISITION HISTORY

1989	Mar	£96,900,000 cash & £26,100,00 loan notes	Outstanding 50% interest in Savacente Ltd
1990	Jan	£18.5m	Outstanding 50% interest in NewMarket Foods Ltd (formerly Haverhill Meat Products Ltd)
1994	Nov	£214m	Consideration for 50% interest in Giant Food Inc
1995	Mar	£166m cash	Home Charm Group PLC
	Aug	£3m cash & £18m 6% loan stock	Objectirevise Ltd

DEPOSITARY RECEIPTS – AMERICAN

Each American Depositary Share represents four ordinary shares.

RIGHTS OF SHARES

VOTING: One vote per share.

Company Report	COMPANY RESEARCH	May 7, 1997

SAINSBURY, J PLC

SHAREHOLDINGS

DIRECTORS' INTERESTS (including family) in the Ordinary shares of the Company at 07-05-96:
BENEFICIAL: D.J. Sainsbury 321,674,572; Others 13,855,473.
NON BENEFICIAL: D.J. Sainsbury 4,903,759; The Rt Hon Sir Timothy Sainsbury MP 66,538,569. OPTIONS: 2,798,775.
MAJOR SHAREHOLDERS in the Company at 09-03-96: Miss J.S. Portrait a partner of Denton Hall, the Company's solicitors and C.T.S. Stone are trustees of various settlements, including charitable settlements. At 07-05-96, the total holdings of the trusts of which the above are trustees amounted to 18% and 6% respectively. As trustees and beneficially D.J. Sainsbury, the Hon S.D. Sainsbury, Lord Sainsbury of Preston Candover and the Rt Hon Sir Timothy Sainsbury MP held 17%, 5%, 4% and 4% respectively.
NUMBER OF SHAREHOLDERS at 09-03-96: 111,012.

DIVIDEND PAYMENT DETAILS –
ORDINARY Year end March 31 (approximately)

		Pence Per Share Gross	Net	Tax %	Millions of Shares	Paid	Holders	Ex Date
1992	aInt	3.2	2.4	25	1,757.6	20-01-92	21-11-91	11-11-91
	aFin	8.467	6.35	25	1,757.6	31-07-92	11-06-92	01-06-92
1993	aInt	3.6	2.7	25	1,764.3	18-01-93	26-11-92	16-11-92
	aFin	9.125	7.3	20	1,774.8	30-07-93	11-06-93	24-05-93
1994	aInt	3.75	3	20	1,790.4	17-01-94	09-12-93	29-11-93
	aFin	9.5	7.6	20	1,790.4	29-07-94	16-06-94	06-06-94
1995	aInt	4	3.2	20	1,806	18-01-95	01-12-94	14-11-94
	aFin	10.625	8.5	20	1,806	28-07-95	09-06-95	22-05-95
1996	aInt	4.25	3.4	20	1,824	17-01-96	21-11-95	13-11-95
	aFin	10.875	8.7	20	1,839	26-07-96	29-05-96	20-05-96

(a) Scrip Option

SCRIP OPTION DETAILS –
ORDINARY Year end March 31 (approximately)

	Basis	Addl Cash Dividend Per Share	Paid	Election Date	Dividend Pence Per Share Foregone
1992	Int 1:146	1.4p	20-01-92	17-12-91	2.39041
	Fin 1:74.26772	–	31-07-92	01-07-92	6.35
1993	Int 1:179.03704	–	18-01-93	30-11-92	2.7
	Fin 1:65.28767	–	30-07-93	05-07-93	7.3
1994	Int 1:135.6	–	17-01-94	31-12-93	3.0
	Fin 1:51.18421	–	29-07-94	06-06-94	7.6
1995	Int 1:130.6875	–	24-02-95	14-11-94	3.2
	Fin 1:51.341176	–	17-11-96	13-11-95	8.5
1996	Int 1:115.05882	–	19-16-96	20-05-96	3.4

DIVIDENDS OF EARLIER YEARS – ORDINARY

Net: 1987, 7p; Cap 100%; 1988, 4.2p; 1989, 5.05p; 1990, 6.10p; 1991, 7.35p

SCRIP OPTIONS OF EARLIER YEARS

1991, Fin 1:72 (plus 2.2p addl cash dividend)

PER SHARE RECORD OF 25p ORDINARY –
Adjusted for Capital Changes

	Mar 14 1992	Mar 13 1993	Mar 12 1994	Mar 11 1995	Mar 09 1996
EARNINGS based on Reported Profits					
Basic – Under FRS3	25.69p	28.5p	8.6p	29.8p	26.8p
Adjusted		b28.5p	b27.6p	29.7p	28.3p
Diluted – Under FRS3	25.22p	27.9p	27.0p	29.0p	26.4p
Adjusted Diluted – Under FRS3	25.34p	b27.9p	b27.0p	29.0p	27.8p
EARNINGS based on Adjusted Profits					
IIMR Headline	25.84p	28.61p	26.72p	29.69p	27.07p
Shares on which earnings calculated (m)					
Basic	a1,705.7	a1,765.9	a1782.1	a1,798.3	a1,817.4
Diluted	a1,815.1	a1,875.0	a1901.7	a1,918.4	a1,933.0
NET DIVIDEND	c8.75p	c10.00p	c10.60p	c11.7p	c12.1p
DIVIDEND COVER	d3.0	d2.9	d2.5	d2.5	d2.2

1 → (IIMR Headline)

5 → (DIVIDEND COVER)

SAINSBURY, J PLC

NET ASSET VALUE					
At B/s date	149.9p	170.7p	169.8p	182.1p	192.9p
Capital Issue Factor	–	–	–	–	–

(a) Estimated weighted average. (b) Before change in accounting depreciation and exceptional administrative expenses. (c) With scrip option. (d) IIMR Headline.

PRICES to December 31 – Adjusted for Capital Changes

LONDON

ORDINARY (pence)	1991	1992	1993	1994	1995
High	388.0	581.0	582.0	478.0	477.0
Low	300.5	337.0	365.0	346.0	367.0

BORROWINGS at 09-03-96

LOAN STOCK
8% IRREDEEMABLE UNSECURED. Issued and Outstanding £3m.
NOTES
9.125% 1996. Outstanding: £98m.
8.5% 2000. Outstanding: £150m.
SHORT TERM. Outstanding: £3m.
OTHER UNSECURED
Outstanding: £29m, including £3m due within one year.
BONDS
8.5% CONVERTIBLE CAPITAL 2005. Issued and Outstanding: £156.0m. Each bond is convertible into 2.5% Exchangeable Redeemable Preference shares of the issuing Company which may be redeemed or exchanged into Ordinary shares of J Sainsbury PLC. Convertible at any time prior to 19-11-2005 and redeemable at their paid-up value or exchangable for Ordinary shares in J Sainsbury PLC at 337p per Ordinary share. The issuing Company is entitled to require conversion on or after 20-11-95 in certain circumstances or if 80% of Bonds have been exchanged. 8.5% 1996 Outstanding: £98m.
BANK LOANS AND OVERDRAFTS
Outstanding: £581m, due within one year.
TERM BANK LOANS
Outstanding £26m.
FINANCE LEASES
Outstanding: £109m, including £8m due within one year.
OTHER LOANS
LOAN TO HOMEBASE LTD FROM MINORITY SHAREHOLDER. Outstanding: £13m. Interest at base rate. Unsecured for terms of 5 years.
SECURED LOANS Outstanding £2m.

CONSENSUS FORECAST

Forecast last revised February 26, 1996

			a Mar 1995	Mar 1996	Mar 1997
Pre Tax Profit	(£m)	LATEST	808.27	784.25	845.00
		High		830.00	928.00
		Low		760.00	800.00
		Previous		825.40	897.00
		Std. Deviation		28.62	49.09
EPS	(Pence)	LATEST	28.92	28.27	30.18
		High		30.10	33.10
		Low		26.90	28.00
		Previous		29.46	31.63
		Std. Deviation		1.22	1.84
EPS Growth		LATEST		(2.20)	6.80
		Previous		12.39	13.64
Dividend	(Pence)	LATEST	9.00	12.25	13.39
		High		12.50	14.10
		Low		12.00	12.90
		Previous		5.00	5.00
		Std. Deviation		0.25	0.44
No of brokers		LATEST		4	4
		Previous		24	43

(a) Actual figures.

Consensus estimates and actuals provided by FIRST CALL INTERNATIONAL

Copyright 1996
Telephone 0171-825-8888 – Fax 0171-608-3514
No responsibility accepted for error or omission
Extel is part of Financial Times Information

Licensed to Extel Financial Limited

Company Report	COMPANY RESEARCH	May 7, 1997

SAINSBURY, J PLC

INTERIM RESULTS

Consolidated Interim Results for 28 weeks (Unaudited)

Profit & Loss Account

	Sep 23 1995	Sep 21 1996	
	£m	£m	
TURNOVER	7.049.0	7,499.0	+6.4
REP OPERATING PROF (LOSS)	474.0	411.0	−13.3
Equity a/c profit (loss)	8.0	12.0	+50.0
Interest payable	(31.0)	(36.0)	+16.1
Inv prop disp gain (loss)	5.0	6.0	+20.0
PROFIT (LOSS) BEFORE TAX	456.0	393.0	−13.8
Tax	(149.0)	(130.0)	−12.8
PROFIT (LOSS) AFTER TAX	307.0	263.0	−14.3
Total minority interest	1.0	–	n/a
NET INCOME (LOSS)	308.0	263.0	−14.6
Dividends	(62.0)	(64.0)	+3.2
RETAINED PROFIT (LOSS)	246.0	199.0	−19.1
Total div per share (p)	3.40000	3.50000	+2.9
Reported EPS (p)	16.99000	14.36000	−15.5
Diluted reported EPS (p)	16.35000	13.73000	−16.0

Balance Sheet

	Sep 23 1995	Sep 21 1996	
	£m	£m	
Tangible assets	5,196.0	5,613.0	+8.0
Financial assets	106.0	144.0	+35.8
FIXED ASSETS	5,302.0	5,757.0	+8.6
Stocks	705.0	712.0	+1.0
Debtors	b 281.0	a 235.0	−16.4
Curr asset investments	14.0	4.0	−71.4
CURRENT ASSETS	1,000.0	951.0	−4.9
TOTAL ASSETS	6,302.0	6,708.0	+6.4
CREDS DUE WITHIN 1 YEAR	d 1,883.0	c 1,767.0	−6.2
Net debt	939.0	1,281.0	+36.4
Other long term liabs	10.0	10.0	–
Provisions	30.0	24.0	−20.0
NET ASSETS (LIABS)	3,500.0	3,674.0	+5.0
SHARE CAPITAL	1,480.0	1,547.0	+4.5
RESERVES	2,000.0	2,127.0	+6.4
SHAREHOLDERS' FUNDS	3,480.0	3,674.0	+5.6
Minorities	20.2	–	n/a

(a) includes ACT recoverable (c) excludes borrowings (b) includes ACT recoverable (d) excludes borrowings

CONSOLIDATED PROFIT AND LOSS ACCOUNT

	Mar 14 1992 £m	Mar 13 1993 £m	Mar 12 1994 £m	Mar 11 1995 £m	Mar 09 1996 £m
Gross turnover	9,202.3	10,269.7	11,223.8	12,065.0	13,499.0
Sales taxes/comms etc	(506.8)	(584.2)	(640.6)	(708.0)	(872.0)
TURNOVER	8,695.5	9,685.5	10,583.2	11,357.0	12,627.0
Cost of sales	(7,826.7)	(8,688.9)	(9.574.5)	(10,241.0)	(11,569.0)
GROSS PROFIT	868.8	996.6	1,008.7	1,116.0	1,058.0
Administration exps	(202.8)	(211.6)	(212.9)	(217.0)	(252.0)
TRADING PROFIT	666.0	785.0	795.8	899.0	806.0
Eqty A/c prof (loss)	1.2	(0.4)	0.5	6.0	19.0
Interest/inv income	116.6	32.7	11.5	13.0	9.0
Interest payable	(103.9)	(23.5)	(20.2)	(49.0)	(68.0)
Other expenses net	(49.4)	(58.6)	(56.3)	(61.0)	(50.0)
Excpl (chgs) profits	(2.5)	(2.4)	(362.5)	1.0	(4.0)
PROFIT BEFORE TAX	628.0	732.8	368.8	809.0	712.0
Tax	(184.5)	(228.8)	(227.3)	(270.0)	(234.0)

Copyright 1996
Telephone 0171-825-8888 – Fax 0171-608-3514
No responsibility accepted for error or omission
Extel is part of Financial Times Information

Licensed to Extel Financial Limited

SAINSBURY, J PLC

	Mar 14 1992	Mar 13 1993	Mar 12 1994	Mar 11 1995	Mar 09 1996
PROFIT AFTER TAX	443.5	504.0	141.5	539.0	478.0
Minority interests	(5.3)	(1.2)	0.1	(4.0)	10.0
NET INCOME	438.2	502.8	141.6	535.0	488.0
Ordinary dividends	(153.7)	(177.3)	(189.6)	(211.0)	(222.0)
RETD PROFITS (LOSSES)	284.5	325.5	(48.0)	324.0	266.0

NOTES TO CONSOLIDATED PROFIT AND LOSS ACCOUNT

	Mar 14 1992	Mar 13 1993	Mar 12 1994	Mar 11 1995	Mar 09 1996
	£m	£m	£m	£m	£m
INTEREST/INV INCOME					
Investment income	–	5.6	–	–	–
Interest income	116.6	27.1	11.5	13.0	9.0
	116.6	32.7	11.5	13.0	9.0
INTEREST PAYABLE					
Int within 5 yrs	(134.1)	(40.9)	(35.5)	(38.0)	(56.0)
Int after 5 yrs	(1.8)	(4.4)	(2.9)	(2.0)	(2.0)
Other int payable	24.5)	(24.3)	(25.8)	(25.0)	(24.0)
Interest capitalised	56.5	46.1	44.0	16.0	14.0
	(103.9)	(23.5)	(20.2)	(49.0)	(68.0)
OTHER EXPENSES NET					
Profit sharing exps	(49.4)	(58.6)	(56.3)	(61.0)	(50.0)
EXCPL (CHGS) PROFITS					
FA disposal gain	(2.5)	(2.4)	7.0	1.0	(4.0)
Fixed assets w/o	–	–	(341.5)	–	–
Reorganisation costs	–	–	(28.0)	–	–
	(2.5)	(2.4)	(362.5)	1.0	(4.0)
TAX BY COUNTRY					
UK corporation tax	(193.3)	(226.3)	(229.9)	(259.0)	(211.0)
Domestic deferred tax	–	0.7	7.5	(2.0)	(3.0)
Associated cos tax	(0.3)	–	–	(3.0)	(8.0)
Domestic tax	(193.6)	(225.6)	(222.4)	(264.0)	(222.0)
Overseas tax	(5.5)	(3.2)	(4.9)	(11.0)	(12.0)
Misc tax by country	14.6	–	–	5.0	–
	(184.5)	(228.8)	(227.3)	(270.0)	(234.0)
TAX BY TYPE					
Current taxation	(199.1)	(232.7)	(240.0)	(270.0)	(223.0)
Deferred taxation	–	3.9	11.6	(2.0)	(3.0)
Prior years tax	–	0.5	1.1	5.0	–
Associated cos tax	(0.3)	(0.5)	–	(3.0)	(8.0)
Misc tax by type	14.9	–	–	–	–
	(184.5)	(228.8)	(227.3)	(270.0)	(234.0)
TAX					
Tax on exceptionals	0.3	–	–	–	–
ORDINARY DIVIDENDS					
Interim ord dividends	(42.0)	(47.6)	(53.5)	(57.0)	(62.0)
Final ord dividends	(111.7)	(129.7)	(136.1)	(154.0)	(160.0)
	(153.7)	(177.3)	(189.6)	(211.0)	(222.0)
RETD PROFITS (LOSSES)					
Parent company	240.1	258.0	(71.8)	273.0	354.0
Subsidiaries	45.4	66.3	23.3	45.0	(107.0)
Equity A/c cos	(1.0)	1.2	0.5	6.0	19.0
	284.5	325.5	(48.0)	324.0	266.0
PROFIT BEFORE TAX is after (charging) crediting					
Directors emoluments	(3.3)	(4.0)	(3.4)	(4.4)	(4.2)
Wages & salaries	(849.3)	(937.6)	(1,022.21)	(1,074.0)	(1,236.0)
Social security	(58.2)	(64.7)	(73.8)	(72.0)	(77.0)
Staff pensions	(31.5)	(33.3)	(36.2)	(38.0)	(42.0)
Profit sharing	–	–	–	(61.0)	(50.0)
Staff expenses	(939.0)	(1,035.6)	(1,132.2)	(1,245.0)	(1,405.0)

Copyright 1996
Telephone 0171-825-8888 – Fax 0171-608-3514
No responsibility accepted for error or omission
Extel is part of Financial Times Information

Licensed to Extel Financial Limited

Company Report | COMPANY RESEARCH | May 7, 1997

SAINSBURY, J PLC

Auditors remuneration	(0.5)	(0.5)	(0.5)	(0.5)	(0.5)
Non-audit fees	(0.2)	(0.7)	(0.6)	(0.7)	(0.6)
Operating leases	(103.7)	(112.0)	(116.2)	(122.0)	(205.0)
Depreciation	(135.6)	(154.7)	(206.9)	(228.0)	(278.0)
Leasing income net	–	–	14.5	17.0	19.0
Reorganisation costs	–	–	–	–	(48.0)
Av no of staff	112,784	76,524	78,974	82,345	95,519

Additional notes to CONSOLIDATED PROFIT AND LOSS ACCOUNT

	Mar 14 1992	Mar 13 1993	Mar 12 1994	Mar 11 1995	Mar 09 1996
	£m	£m	£m	£m	£m
OPERATING LEASES					
Plant & machinery	(7.2)	(8.5)	(9.3)	(9.0)	(11.0)
Other	(96.5)	(103.5)	(106.9)	(113.0)	(194.0)
	(103.7)	(112.0)	(116.2)	(122.0)	(205.0)
DEPRECIATION					
Owned assets	(133.9)	(150.7)	(202.8)	(224.0)	(270.0)
Leased assets	(1.7)	(4.0)	(4.1)	(4.0)	(8.0)
	(135.6)	(154.7)	(206.9)	(228.0)	(278.0)

CONSOLIDATED PROFIT AND LOSS ACCOUNT Continuing – Acquired

	Mar 11 1995	Mar 09 1996
	£m	£m
TURNOVER	–	577
Cost of sales	–	(620)
GROSS LOSS	–	(43)
Administration exps	–	(15)
TRADING LOSS	–	(58)

BUSINESS ANALYSIS – Turnover

	Mar 14 1992	Mar 13 1993	Mar 12 1994	Mar 11 1995	Mar 09 1996
	£m	£m	£m	£m	£m
Food retailing	8,935.4	9,976.6	10,837.8	10,989.0	11,663.0
DIY retailing	257.6	282.8	328.0	321.0	940.0
Property development	–	–	39.9	30.0	19.0
Food manufacturing	9.3	10.3	18.1	117.0	118.0
VAT	(506.8)	(584.2)	(640.6)	–	–
Intragroup Sales	–	–	–	(100.0)	(113.0)
	8,695.5	9,685.5	10,583.2	11,357.0	12,627.0

BUSINESS ANALYSIS – Profit before tax

	Mar 14 1992	Mar 13 1993	Mar 12 1994	Mar 11 1995	Mar 09 1996
	£m	£m	£m	£m	£m
Food retailing	652.1	770.8	766.4	865.0	830.0
DIY retailing	15.3	17.8	22.6	31.0	(22.0)
Property development	–	–	8.0	6.0	3.0
Food manufacturing	(1.4)	(3.6)	(1.2)	(3.0)	(5.0)
Associates	1.2	(0.4)	0.5	6.0	19.0
Profit sharing	(49.4)	(58.6)	(56.3)	(60.0)	(50.0)
Excpl admin exps	–	–	(369.5)	–	–
Property disposals	(2.5)	(2.4)	7.0	1.0	(4.0)
Net Interest	12.7	9.2	(8.7)	(36.0)	(59.0)
	628.0	732.8	368.8	809.0	712.0

BUSINESS ANALYSIS – Net assets

	Mar 14 1992	Mar 13 1993	Mar 12 1994	Mar 11 1995	Mar 09 1996
	£m	£m	£m	£m	£m
Food Retailing	2,909.8	3,406.3	3,526.2	3,708.0	4,276.0
DIY Retailing	157.6	165.3	153.4	154.0	320.0
Property development	–	19.7	32.4	16.0	30.0
Food manufacturing	45.8	24.6	23.3	24.0	17.0
Net Borrowings	(456.1)	(569.8)	(678.5)	(592.0)	(1,098.0)
	2,657.1	3,046.1	3,056.8	3,310.0	3,545.0

SAINSBURY, J PLC

GEOGRAPHICAL ANALYSIS – Turnover by source

	Mar 14 1992	Mar 13 1993	Mar 12 1994	Mar 11 1995	Mar 09 1996
	£m	£m	£m	£m	£m
UK	8,159.2	9,179.1	9,909.3	10,123.0	11,291.0
USA	1,043.1	1,090.6	1,314.5	1,334.0	1,449.0
Intra-group & VAT	(506.8)	(584.2)	(640.6)	(100.0)	(113.0)
	8,695.5	9,685.5	10,583.2	11,357.0	12,627.0

GEOGRAPHICAL ANALYSIS – Profit before tax

	Mar 14 1992	Mar 13 1993	Mar 12 1994	Mar 11 1995	Mar 09 1996
	£m	£m	£m	£m	£m
UK	645.4	766.4	764.8	859.0	755.0
USA	20.6	18.6	31.0	40.0	51.0
Net other expenses	(36.0)	(52.2)	(427.0)	(61.0)	(50.0)
Exceptional chgs	–	–	–	1.0	(4.0)
Assoc co profit	–	–	–	6.0	19.0
Net interest exp	–	–	–	(36.0)	(59.0)
	628.0	732.8	368.8	809.0	712.0

GEOGRAPHICAL ANALYSIS – Net assets

	Mar 14 1992	Mar 13 1993	Mar 12 1994	Mar 11 1995	Mar 09 1996
	£m	£m	£m	£m	£m
UK	2,856.8	3,256.3	3,374.8	3,564.0	4,206.0
USA	256.4	359.6	360.5	338.0	437.0
Net borrowings	(456.1)	(569.8)	(678.5)	(592.0)	(1,098.0)
	2,657.1	3,046.1	3,056.8	3,310.0	3,545.0

CONSOLIDATED STATEMENT OF CASH FLOWS

	Mar 14 1992	Mar 13 1993	Mar 12 1994	Mar 11 1995	Mar 09 1996
	£m	£m	£m	£m	£m
OPERATING ACTIVITIES	787.1	973.2	990.9	1,070.0	1,012.0
INVESTMENT RETURN AND SERVICING OF FINANCE					
Assoc cos divs recd	–	–	–	–	5.0
Interest received	111.2	35.1	10.9	13.0	11.0
Interest paid	(144.6)	(71.5)	(72.2)	(77.0)	(82.0)
Dividends paid ord	(115.1)	(132.1)	(154.0)	(169.0)	(208.0)
Other servicing infl	(6.9)	–	–	–	–
	(155.4)	(168.5)	(215.3)	(233.0)	(274.0)
TAXATION					
Domestic tax paid	(124.9)	(171.8)	(210.8)	(208.0)	(261.0)
Overseas tax paid	(6.8)	(7.6)	(9.0)	(13.0)	(10.0)
	(131.7)	(179.4)	(219.8)	(221.0)	(271.0)
INVESTING ACTIVITIES					
Subsidiaries acqd	–	–	(3.1)	–	(321.0)
Assoc cos acqd	(6.0)	—	(0.1)	(207.0)	(4.0)
Invests acquired	(190.9)	–	–	–	(4.0)
Tangibles acquired	(707.6)	(741.7)	(748.0)	(494.0)	(709.0)
Assoc cos sold	–	0.4	–	–	–
Investments sold	–	109.7	75.8	7.0	–
Tangibles sold	72.1	50.5	47.8	33.0	50.0
	(832.4)	(581.1)	(627.6)	(661.0)	(988.0)
NET CASH FLOW BEFORE FINANCING	(332.4)	44.2	(71.8)	(45.0)	(521.0)
FINANCING					
Long term debt raised	93.0	86.1	20.6	98.0	182.0
Share capital issued	509.8	18.2	10.7	14.0	22.0
Long term debt repaid	(144.8)	(111.8)	(10.8)	(111.0)	(31.0)
Finance leases repaid	(0.5)	(0.7)	(1.0)	(1.0)	(6.0)
Issue expenses	(6.1)	–	(0.4)	–	–
	451.4	(8.2)	19.1	–	167.0

Copyright 1996
Telephone 0171-825-8888 – Fax 0171-608-3514
No responsibility accepted for error or omission
Extel is part of Financial Times Information

Company Report   COMPANY RESEARCH   May 7, 1997

SAINSBURY, J PLC

CASH INCR (DECR)	119.0	36.0	(52.7)	(45.0)	(354.0)
Currency appreciation	–	0.4	(0.1)	(1.0)	1.0
B/S CASH INCR (DECR)	119.0	36.4	(52.8)	(46.0)	(353.0)

NOTES TO CONSOLIDATED STATEMENT OF CASH FLOWS

	Mar 14 1992	Mar 13 1993	Mar 12 1994	Mar 11 1995	Mar 09 1996
	£m	£m	£m	£m	£m
OPERATING ACTIVITIES					
Trading profit	666.0	785.0	795.8	899.0	806.0
Depn & amortn incr	135.6	154.7	206.9	228.0	270.0
Asset disposal	–	–	–	2.0	3.0
Provision increases	–	–	–	(4.0)	45.0
Other tdg adj incr	(49.4)	(58.6)	(57.4)	(61.0)	(50.0)
Decrease in stocks	(1.5)	(48.0)	(7.2)	(53.0)	(103.0)
Decrease in debtors	4.7	(22.1)	(24.3)	(14.0)	24.0
Increase in creditors	31.7	162.2	77.1	100.0	38.0
Other wkg cap decr	–	–	–	(27.0)	(21.0)
	787.1	973.2	990.9	1,070.0	1,012.0

CONSOLIDATED BALANCE SHEETS

	Mar 14 1992	Mar 13 1993	Mar 12 1994	Mar 11 1995	Mar 09 1996
	£m	£m	£m	£m	£m
FIXED ASSETS					
Tangible assets	3,809.2	4,448.5	4,641.5	4,852.0	5,458.0
Financial assets	27.6	29.4	18.0	98.0	117.0
	3,836.8	4,477.9	4,659.5	4,950.0	5,575.0
CURRENT ASSETS					
Stocks	386.5	448.2	460.0	509.0	761.0
Trade debtors	15.7	21.8	55.2	31.0	52.0
Prepayments	16.3	20.8	20.3	42.0	46.0
ACT recoverable	37.3	37.6	34.0	38.0	40.0
Tax recoverable	0.9	0.7	–	–	–
Other debtors	47.9	52.0	37.5	61.0	66.0
Cash & equivalents	173.9	144.4	171.3	199.0	209.0
Notes, bills & invs	189.6	78.5	52.7	2.0	5.0
	868.1	804.0	831.0	882.0	1,179.0
CREDS due within 1 yr					
Short term debt	249.0	88.1	300.5	231.0	809.0
Trade creditors	578.5	682.4	712.3	725.0	816.0
Accruals	70.9	73.2	81.2	95.0	152.0
Revenue tax	187.1	225.0	225.1	265.0	216.0
Tax & social security	20.6	31.2	30.9	32.0	47.0
Dividends	111.9	129.7	136.1	154.0	160.0
Other creditors	250.2	295.0	296.8	334.0	319.0
	1,468.2	1,524.6	1,782.9	1,836.0	2,519.0
NET CURRENT LIABS	(600.1)	(720.6)	(951.9)	(954.0)	(1,340.0)
TOTAL ASSETS LESS CURRENT LIABILITIES	3,236.7	3,757.3	3,707.6	3,996.0	4,235.0
CREDS due after 1 yr					
Long term debt	570.5	704.6	602.0	659.0	617.0
Other L/T liabs	7.4	8.6	8.7	10.0	19.0
	577.9	713.2	610.7	669.0	636.0
PROVISIONS	1.7	(2.0)	40.1	17.0	54.0
NET ASSETS	2,657.1	3,046.1	3,056.8	3,310.0	3,545.0
Ordinary shares	439.4	443.7	447.6	452.0	458.0
Share premium	837.5	895.4	949.9	1,000.0	1,074.0
Revaluation reserves	26.8	26.8	32.7	39.0	43.0
Retained earnings	1,337.2	1,662.8	1,609.3	1,798.0	1,959.0
SHAREHOLDERS' FUNDS	2,640.9	3,028.7	3,039.5	3,289.0	3,534.0
Minority interests	16.2	17.4	17.3	21.0	11.0
NET ASSETS	2,657.1	3,046.1	3,056.8	3,310.0	3,545.0

4

SAINSBURY, J PLC

NOTES TO CONSOLIDATED BALANCE SHEETS

	Mar 14 1992	Mar 13 1993	Mar 12 1994	Mar 11 1995	Mar 09 1996
	£m	£m	£m	£m	£m
TANGIBLE ASSETS					
Property – cost	–	3,456.3	3,933.1	–	4,784.0
Property – valn	–	109.0	101.8	–	94.0
Property cost/valn	2,897.9			4,341.0	
Property depreciation	(97.8)	(125.6)	(479.6)	(518.0)	(654.0)
Property NBV	2,800.1	3,439.7	3,555.3	3,823.0	4,224.0
Oth tangible FA-cost		1,552.1	1,746.2	1,988.0	2,458.0
Oth tang FA cost/valn	1,345.7		–		
Oth tangible FA depn	(561.8)	(677.7)	(807.6)	(959.0)	(1,224.0)
Other tangible FA NBV	783.9	874.4	938.6	1,029.0	1,234.0
Cap w-i-p NBV c/f	225.2	134.4	147.6	–	–
Tangible assets	3,809.2	4,448.5	4,641.5	4,852.0	5,458.0
Cost of land/bldgs	3,084.1	3,648.4	3,123.3	3,749.0	4,835.0
Tang leased assets	56.2	70.3	68.5	59.0	75.0
FINANCIAL ASSETS					
Assoc company loans	–	7.9	1.9	–	–
Invs in assoc cos	20.9	11.7	15.2	97.0	114.0
Other trade invs	6.7	9.8	0.9	1.0	3.0
Trade investments	27.6	29.4	18.0	98.0	117.0
STOCKS					
Land	24.3	33.3	35.3	40.0	62.0
Finished gds & resale	362.2	414.9	424.7	469.0	699.0
	386.5	448.2	460.0	509.0	761.0
DEBTORS includes					
Due after one year	3.3	0.7	7.0	7.0	16.0
DEBT BY TYPE					
Convertible loans	–	200.0	200.0	200.0	156.0
Mortgage loans	–	0.6	–	–	–
Loan capital	3.7	312.1	378.8	325.0	539.0
Bank loans	–	–	64.5	52.0	26.0
Intra-group loans	6.3	7.2	7.6	–	–
Finance leases & HP	62.9	81.4	83.0	77.0	109.0
Bank lns & overdrafts	133.4	143.2	153.8	221.0	581.0
Bills & notes	–	30.7	–	–	–
Other loans	613.2	17.5	14.8	15.0	15.0
	819.2	792.7	902.5	890.0	1,426.0
DEBT BY MATURITY					
Short term loans	108.3	70.7	300.5	231.0	809.0
Debt due within 1 yr	140.7	17.4	–	–	–
Short term debt	249.0	88.1	300.5	231.0	809.0
Due within 1 to 2 yrs	–	109.7	8.8	193.0	168.0
Due within 2 to 5 yrs	–	267.7	275.9	191.0	203.0
Due after 5 years	–	327.2	317.3	275.0	246.0
Due after 1 year	570.5	–	–	–	–
	819.5	792.7	902.5	890.0	1,426.0
DEBT BY SECURITY					
Secured	70.1	84.6	85.0	79.0	111.0
Unsecured	743.1	708.1	56.7	135.0	172.0
Misc debt by backing	6.3	–	760.8	676.0	1,143.0
	819.5	792.7	902.5	890.0	1,426.0
PROVISIONS					
Deferred taxation	1.7	(2.0)	(13.6)	(6.0)	(32.0)
Other provisions	–	–	53.7	23.0	86.0
	1.7	(2.0)	40.1	17.0	54.0

SAINSBURY, J PLC

COMMITMENTS AND CONTINGENCIES					
Capital contracted	418.5	416.9	347.4	268.0	247.0
Cap not contracted	430.8	478.9	398.3	459.0	–
Optg leases-property	101.2	104.5	83.6	118.0	192.0
Optg leases – other	9.7	8.6	6.7	9.0	10.0

DIRECTORS' REPORT

FIXED ASSETS. The Directors believe that the aggregate open market value of Group properties exceeds net book value of £4,224.0m by a considerable margin.

CHAIRMAN'S STATEMENT

OUTLOOK. In the past year we have improved the competitive position of Sainsbury's supermarkets, strengthened its rate of expansion and reinforced its top management structure. These changes will take time to translate fully into improved performance. Further innovation and development of our offer is under way and we are moving decisively forward. Looking beyond our main supermarket business, Savacentre provides us with a strong distinctive format with substantial growth potential. Shaw's is expanding rapidly and profitably and the integration of Texas into Homebase is a major opportunity to increase profits. These businesses will add significantly to the earnings growth of the Group in the years ahead.

ANNUAL GENERAL MEETING (52 weeks to 09-03-96)

The Queen Elizabeth II Conference Centre, Broad Sanctuary, Westminster, London, SW1P 3EE, July 3 at noon.

FINANCIAL CALENDAR

Interim Report 30th October 1996; Preliminary Figures 7th May 1997; Annual General Meeting 6th July 1997.

PROFIT (LOSS) BEFORE TAX

You may think that this indicator, shown as (2) in Figure 10.1, should be the most important one and should take precedent over EPS. Well, yes, it is important, but making profits is only one of the tasks confronting good management. Keeping costs down is another.

An item in the *Profit and Loss Account* which is chargeable to pre-tax profits is one called 'minority interests'. This is any profit (credit) or loss (debit) which the company must declare to its shareholders – and remember that it may have financial obligations if the loss is considerable. A minority interest is one where the company owns less than 50 per cent of the issued capital of another company. If it owned more than 50 per cent, then the company would become a subsidiary, and its figures would be incorporated in the main company's consolidated accounts. It is perfectly possible for a company to make increasing pre-tax profits which are eroded by corresponding increases in losses attributable to minority interests. It is possible, but unlikely, and if you saw such a situation it would be a pretty poor reflection on the management.

If the pre-tax profits are fluctuating, you should dig a bit deeper into the figures and look at such items as wages, salaries (particularly those of the directors), interest charges, turnover and stock levels. Compare one year's figures with another, and telephone the company secretary and ask him why such items appear to be tolerated since they are having an adverse effect on the profits. Obviously you would not buy a share in a company which has a record of falling pre-tax profits.

TRADING PROFIT (LOSS)

This indicator, shown as (3) in Figure 10.1, is exactly what it says it is, trading profit, sometimes referred to as 'gross profit'. In essence, they are the difference between the revenue received for goods or services sold and the cost of producing them. If you want to do the sums, you can express the trading profits as a percentage of turnover and find out the gross margin which the company is making on its sales. This exercise is really relevant only if you are going to compare the margins achieved between two or more companies in the same business. You might, for example, compare the margins of Sainsbury and Tesco; you would not compare Tesco with Barclays Bank.

If the trading profit is increasing, and at the same time the pre-tax profit is falling, then there are certainly some questions to be answered. In addition to those suggested above, you might look to see whether there have been any substantial increases in leasing charges or bank overdraft costs or any other substantial increase in the liabilities of the company. Good management should be able to make steadily increasing profits without any unproportional increase in the costs of achieving the growth.

SHAREHOLDERS' FUNDS

This figure, sometimes called 'Reserves' in the balance sheet, and shown as (4) in Figure 10.1, shows the retained profits over the years which are attributable to the shareholders of the company. They should be increasing steadily, year after year. If they are not, then the reason will be that the company is paying out more in dividends to its shareholders than it is earning, and if this trend continues, it is very bad news indeed.

The pressures on companies to increase their annual dividends to shareholders, or at worst to maintain the same level as last year, are immense. This is the second important item that the market takes into consideration when deciding whether to support the company or not. It is the main factor which contributes to the reputation of the City being interested in short-term results only. To a great extent I have to agree with the criticism, but the pension funds and insurance companies and unit and investment trusts which are dedicated to providing high income for their clients or unit holders are the major shareholders in the market place and they wield a lot of clout. Consequently, many chairmen feel that they would rather maintain the approbation of the City and pay out increased dividends at the expense of the shareholders' funds reserve, even though the company has not earned a sufficient amount so to do.

The only exceptions to this rule are property companies which are obliged to distribute all their earnings. Nevertheless, property companies apart, if you see payments being made by way of dividends for more than one year, and there are not enough earnings to cover them, my advice is to get out of the share if you hold it, or to avoid buying it if you don't. Paying out dividends without earnings cover is very bad news because if the practice is maintained, the company will go broke. It is always a sign of bad management.

DIVIDEND COVER

This item, shown in Figure 10.1, as (5) is the quick check on what is happening to the shareholders' funds, described above. The figure represents the number of times the dividends are covered by earnings. Ideally, the figure should be in the region of 2. If you see the figure at less than 1 then be alerted to the dangers described above. Prudent management will be able to increase dividends as well as to increase the dividend cover at the same time, thus increasing the amount held in shareholders' funds.

RETURN ON CAPITAL EMPLOYED (ROCE)

For the long-term investor, this indicator is probably the best one for showing how good or bad the management is at running the company. It shows the gross 'yield' on the shareholders' funds that the management is able to extract from its sales of its products. It is not shown in the Extel card and you have to do the calculation yourself. It is a very simple one and all you have to do is to divide the trading profit (sometimes called the 'operating profit'), by the shareholders' funds, and multiply the result by 100. The ROCE is expressed as a percentage. You should do this exercise every year for the last five years and watch the trend that the figures throw up.

A falling trend will indicate reducing profit margins on the sales of the products, if the annual sales figures are not decreasing. In other words, the company is making less profit per £1 of sales than it did a year ago. Such a picture usually means that the company is cutting the prices of its goods to meet increased competition.

If that is the case, have a look at the amount spent in research and development, if it is the sort of company which has to continue to produce new products to maintain its share of the market. This is likely to apply to most manufacturing companies, not so much to pure retailers. It applies particularly to drug and electronic goods companies, such as computer manufacturers.

> 'A falling trend will indicate reducing profit margins on the sales of the product, if the annual sales figures are not decreasing.'

If the sales figures are themselves decreasing, then unless the company has some pretty good plans to recover its market share, or to open up new markets, any investment here is probably going to mean that you will lose your capital. It is only a question of how soon it will be before you kiss goodbye to your money.

SUMMARY

In this chapter we have described in some detail:

- the six key indicators which anyone managing investments should monitor constantly;
- where to find the relevant data from the company Extel card;
- how to interpret the progression of the figures under each heading;
- why these key indicators are so important.

THE INFLUENCE OF POLITICS ON THE MARKET

INTRODUCTION

In this chapter we examine:

- how the government attempts to balance its books
- how the government funds income deficit
- the effects of inflation
- the effects inflation has on current and future interest rates
- how interest rates affect the exchange rates
- the effects of changing taxation.

It is not simply a coincidence that Oxford University runs a degree course combining philosophy, politics and economics, sometimes referred to as 'Modern Greats'. The constituent parts are inextricably linked, and it would be foolish to think that the long-term investor can ignore politics or simply fail to consider the influence which governments have on stockmarkets and the degree to which political and economic matters influence share prices. It is an enormous subject and many books have been written about it, while the quality newspapers and journals devote considerable space in every issue to attempts to analyse the possible and probable effects of government action on share prices, interest rates, exchange rates and taxation.

Since the subject is so big, and being aware that the average investor has a limited time to read the Press each day, I shall confine myself to explaining the main points of concern and the reasons why they matter.

I am often asked whether I think that the market is going to go up or down by clients who have just as much access to published information as I do. As I have said before in this book, investing in shares is very largely a matter of applied commonsense, as well as reading as much as you can and storing up knowledge in your memory.

The Press is always full of comment and predictions about any intentions which the chancellor of the exchequer of the day may be set to announce, or thought to be about to announce. If you ask the same question of six different economists you will get six different answers. The same thing goes for analysts and stockbrokers and any other 'experts' you care to nominate. The point is that *you* have to make the final decision to buy or to sell because it is *your money* that is at risk.

It is always a good thing to remember the basics and think your way through the ways in which the economy is managed and what affects the stockmarket.

INCOME TAX

The government receives income from tax. It has to pay out money for social security, the armed forces, pensions, the civil service, the judiciary, welfare of various kinds and so on. The bill is huge and usually the amount going out exceeds the amount coming in. You may have strong views, as I do, about the welfare policies, but unless radical changes are made it is unlikely that income and outgoings will be brought into balance and remain so permanently, so to make up the deficit the government either has to raise taxes, or borrow money. The sums needed are called the public sector borrowing requirement (PSBR), and recently it was soaking up in excess of £30 billion per annum. Raising taxes has one major drawback. It is a slow way to cover the deficit because the government bills have to be paid daily and any increase in tax will not produce extra income for some time.

> 'It is always a good thing to remember the basics and think your way through the ways in which the economy is managed and what affects the stockmarket.'

GILT ISSUES

The government, through the Bank of England, raises the money by issuing gilts at auction. The gilts are issued carrying a fixed interest coupon, payable every six months throughout their life and they are issued with a date on which they will be redeemed at 100. The period, which is set at the outset, may run for anything between five and 20 years. It is the job of the Bank to assess what level of interest it is reasonable to assume will be attractive to the market without giving too much away. Obviously the Bank wants to raise as much money as it can whilst paying as little as possible and the task calls for fine judgement. The Bank has to set the rate of interest today (when interest rates might be high) which will be an extra part of the government's annual outgoings for the next 20 years. At the same time it has to take into consideration the strong probability that interest rates will not remain high during the life of the gilt, so it has to pick a rate of interest which will not become a burden in the future but which will still be sufficiently high to attract investors under current circumstances.

If the current rate of interest is, say 6.75 per cent, and the Bank offers £1 billion of gilts for redemption in the year 2017 with a coupon of 6 per cent, then it will probably receive only about 85 per cent of the money it wants, because the investors will bid a price for the stock which will give them a current yield equivalent to other existing investment opportunities in the market with similar risk. So to raise the money which the government requires, an awful lot of stock has to be issued, and some of the proceeds will probably have to pay for previous loans which are due to mature, so the results of government profligacy become an ever increasing burden of debt to be discharged in the future.

Thus when you see the volume of gilt issues rising, it is a sign of potential future inflation.

STRENGTH OF STERLING

The next factor to consider is the question of the strength of sterling. If the pound is strong against other currencies, i.e., you can get more French francs, US dollars, D-marks, yen or whatever, for £1 than you could previously, whilst it may be excellent for people going on holidays abroad, British exporters of goods and services find that they are becoming uncompetitive in the international market place. Now one of the reasons for sterling's strength is that the rate of interest which foreign institutions such as banks and managed investment funds can obtain in the UK is greater than they can get domestically. They will be attracted to safe guaranteed government bonds such as gilts.

Consequently if UK government stocks have to carry a relatively high coupon because interest rates in Britain are likely to remain high, or possibly go even higher for domestic reasons, not only will the pound remain strong, but perhaps it will get even stronger and so make life even more difficult for those UK companies which rely heavily on overseas markets for the greater part of their earnings.

INFLATION

Inflation is the killer of prosperity. It devalues everything from property to pensions and it was what brought Hitler to power in Germany in the 1930s. Money in Germany was worth 20 to 30 per cent less in the afternoon than it had been in the morning, and this erosion of value continued day after day. It is because of this experience that the Bundesbank has refused to take any chances with their currency or interest rate levels which might lead to an increase in the rate of inflation in any way.

The difference between the Bundesbank and the Bank of England is that the Bundesbank is completely independent from the politicians. The government may want to increase interest rates for all sorts of good sound reasons and the money markets may be urging them to do so, but perhaps because an election is imminent, they defer taking any action to the detriment of the exchange rates. The Bank of England was controlled by the politicians for many years until now. It remains to be seen whether the Bank will be strong enough to resist government pressure in the future, now that it has been made independent.

Inflation is caused by wage costs which are too high; too much money being spent on imported goods; too much money chasing up house prices and too much credit being made available: the 'buy now – pay later' syndrome getting out of hand. You can see some evidence of the rise in inflation from the progress of the retail prices index (RPI). For the last 12 months this figure has been falling to record levels not seen since before the 1939–1945 war. Wage inflation has remained almost static since the end of 1996 and raw material prices have been unchanged for the last 12 months. The performance of this latter index is a direct reflection of a strong pound. Good for manufacturing prices and imported goods but not good for re-exports or exporting British manufactured goods. If there is too much money being spent on goods in the shops, and if those goods that are being bought by the public are imported goods rather than those manufactured in Britain, that is inflationary.

So if the government or the Bank believes that inflation is beginning to rear its ugly head and the rate is expected to accelerate, then they really only have two weapons to use. They can raise interest rates, or taxes, or both. Of course they *could* cut spending on welfare, social security benefits, the armed forces, reduce the number of civil servants employed, or introduce a pay freeze throughout Britain. But it would be political suicide to do so, and with the rules and restrictions imposed from Brussels under the edicts from the European Parliament such courses of action would almost certainly contravene the Social Chapter or some such law.

BEAR MARKETS

I have said earlier on in this book that the one thing guaranteed to make any stockmarket reduce prices is uncertainty. Uncertainty equals doubt. Doubt equals fear of loss. The immediate reaction to fear of loss is to sell investments in case the capital value falls away or disappears. Put yourself in the shoes of the market makers; they are in business to make money just as much as any investor and the moment that they sense a feeling of uncertainty they will reduce share prices and go on doing so until the sellers refuse to take huge losses and say to themselves that they would rather wait for the prices to recover before dumping any more shares.

The stockmarket is a finely tuned machine and it reacts very quickly to good and bad news. It abounds with rumours all the time, but its sources of information are pretty good and it is adept at checking up on the progress of most of the companies whose shares are traded on the market. The traders are fairly cynical about political rhetoric and public avowals of providing full employment and increased benefits for one and all. They can do their sums as well as anybody and if it seems to them that any government is pursuing policies which will affect corporate earnings adversely for any reason, they will become uneasy and uncertain.

> '... even the best management finds it difficult to deliver the goods if political intervention is unexpected ...'

Don't forget that the share prices today are reflecting the market expectations of earnings six months ahead. Any change in corporate taxation which might affect future earnings to the detriment of shareholders will hit current prices to a greater or lesser extent depending on how long it might take for any loss to be compensated, or until fund managers have adjusted to a reduction in income. Under such circumstances it would be impossible to guess how long it might take for the market to regain the price levels which it was enjoying before such changes were imposed.

At the beginning of Part 2 of this book, I described the necessity for research into individual companies and what aspects to examine; and I would emphasise the importance of satisfying yourself that the chief executive is well-experienced in the business and has a good grip on the management. You will have realised the importance of good-quality products and the need to assure yourself that the company is well-placed to continue to increase its earnings in the future. These are all evidence of good management practice, and when everything is right and under control, you can smell it!

However, even the best management finds it difficult to deliver the goods if political intervention is unexpected and particularly if the actions taken by government, wherever it may be based, increase taxation or the cost of money, or both. When share prices fall, it makes raising money for expansion more difficult and more expensive, with the result that the expansion which was being contemplated may well be postponed or abandoned. Price stability, including the cost of wages and money, leads to bull markets and rising share prices but uncertainty and lack of confidence in the management of the economy results in bear markets and falling share prices.

SUMMARY

In this chapter we have illustrated how:

- political influence can have a dramatic effect on the fixed interest market;
- how a change in the base rates can affect the competitiveness of British exports and thus threaten or boost company earnings;
- how changes in taxation will affect future earnings and possibly alter the emphasis of investment by institutional and managed funds;
- government intervention can introduce doubt and uncertainty into the market with possible dire consequences.

THE USE OF INSURANCE TO COVER INHERITANCE TAX LIABILITIES

INTRODUCTION

In this chapter we explain:

- the role of insurance to cover liability to inheritance tax
- how to calculate what the liability might amount to
- how the payment of liability and the granting of probate are linked
- the importance of writing an insurance policy in trust
- the dangers and costs of transferring current assets into offshore trusts
- the difference between term and whole of life assurance.

LEGAL LIABILITIES

When a death occurs, quite apart from the trauma it generates among those closely related to the deceased, there are some fairly unpleasant laws which apply to the estate and of which most people are unaware.

The first is that all assets of the deceased are frozen until probate has been agreed, which can take months, and the assets include any money in a bank or building society account which are held in the sole name of the person who has died. Such restriction does not apply to deposit or current accounts which are held in joint names between husband and wife, although even with this precaution having been taken, difficulties can arise under certain circumstances.

The first thing to remember is that there is no liability to inheritance tax between husband and wife, at the time of writing, and consequently you should not be pressurised by anyone, be it insurance salesman or bank manager (nowadays it is sometimes difficult to discern the difference between the two), into taking out an insurance policy to cover large sums of benefit if both spouses are alive.

The real problems arise when either the last surviving spouse dies, or both spouses die simultaneously in some accident or disaster. Under these circumstances, the executors of the estate have to pay the Inland Revenue such tax as may be due (which can be a considerable amount of money) without being able to realise cash by selling securities or any other asset until probate has been granted. As you will realise, the banks reap considerable rewards from this rule.

I have known instances when the amount due to be paid to the Inland Revenue was in excess of £50,000 which had to be borrowed for nearly a year before probate was agreed, although there was a portfolio considerably in excess of that figure which could not be touched until the payment had been made. In the meantime the stockmarket had fallen and by the time the assets were released, the value of the portfolio had diminished. There is no redress against such a contingency.

> '... there is no liability to inheritance tax between husband and wife ...'

IS INSURANCE NECESSARY?

Before answering this question, let us look at where the liabilities arise and try to quantify them.

Under current legislation, there is a sum of £215,000 allowed free of inheritance tax for a deceased estate. Remember that this figure applies to the total value of the estate, including any real estate, jewellery, pictures, cars, stocks and shares and anything else of value which belonged to the deceased. Since there is no liability to inheritance tax between husband and wife, this tax free concession applies only when the death of the last survivor occurs. However, it is worth remembering that any stock or shares which are registered jointly between husband and wife can not be sold until probate has been granted. When this has been approved, a sealed copy of the probate must be delivered to the Registrar. Certified copies are not acceptable. A death certificate only registers a death; probate designates who is empowered to sign share transfer forms.

> Any insurance policy which is not written in trust forms part of the estate and so the proceeds will be frozen along with the rest of the assets in the estate until probate has been granted.

This point is very important because the whole object of taking out an insurance policy to cover liabilities to inheritance tax is to provide cash to pay the tax after probate has been agreed but before it is granted. It is only upon the granting of the probate, i.e. when the tax has been paid, that the assets become unfrozen and can be sold.

Any insurance being contemplated *must* be written in trust and if it is, then the benefits of the policy become protected immediately from any liability to inheritance tax because they are deemed to be outside the estate.

Do not confuse the concept of having an insurance policy written in trust with the often vaunted practice of putting your estate or capital investments in stocks and shares into a trust. There is a vast difference between the two and there are many hazards in the short term which are attached to the latter.

An insurance policy which is written in trust can be put into effect immediately with any reputable life assurance company, and they have all the administrative arrangements in place which comply with all the legal requirements to be acceptable to the Inland Revenue. Apart from signing a form which appoints the company as trustees and paying the appropriate premium, there is nothing else for you to do. It does not have to be written offshore anywhere, nor does it require you to change your residence or domicile or make any changes to your normal life. Since there will be no income arising out of such a policy, you will not benefit in any way from making the arrangement whilst you are living. Upon your death, if you are the last survivor, the trustees will make the funds available immediately to the beneficiaries of your will. It is the executors who will be faced with having to pay the inheritance tax, and since it is usual to appoint one or more of the beneficiaries as executors to the estate, they will have access to cash arising out of the policy to meet the cost of the tax.

Dangers of transferring assets into a trust

Transferring assets into a trust for the purpose of avoiding inheritance tax is a whole different ball game, as they say, and there are many dangers in the short-term which can make the entire exercise a waste of time and cost quite a lot of money. It is a move which can involve considerable fees to solicitors and accountants and it will undoubtedly cost a lot to set up. I do not intend to deal with this complicated subject in any detail except to enumerate some of the main areas about which you should be aware.

First, to place any investments or fixed assets such as property in a trust, whether it be within the UK or abroad, will cost a great deal. It is not simply a question of transferring ownership from one person to another or to a trustee. The Inland Revenue deems that if you do this, you have made a disposal of the asset at current market value and if you have held the asset for some years, there will be capital gains tax (CGT) to pay. *You* have to pay it, not the new trust.

Second, the liability to inheritance tax will diminish over a seven-year period from the time that the asset was transferred into the trust. This means to say that although you will have gone to considerable expense to set up the trust *and* possibly had to pay out large sums in CGT, you will not have escaped all liability to inheritance tax until you have survived for seven years after the transfer.

Third, when you set up the trust and transfer the assets into it, you will lose all benefit of income arising from the assets within the trust. You can not set up a trust and be a beneficiary as well. You can be a trustee which means that you can control the investments within the trust, but you cannot receive any income or capital payment from the trust.

If you repatriate any money from the trust at any time during your lifetime for your own benefit, then the Inland Revenue will not accept that the assets of the trust are separate from your own for inheritance tax purposes.

There are many other considerations to be faced if you are contemplating going down this road, and it is essential to get professional advice before you commit yourself. An added hazard is the fact that governments change the laws from time to time, and until the first period of seven years (under current legislation) has passed, you could find that further obstacles were created which might defeat the whole object if you were to die before the arrangements became bombproof.

As a rule of thumb, it is probably not worth contemplating the creation of an offshore trust for any capital sum of less than £500,000 and that you are able to forgo any income which would normally arise from the capital without inhibiting your lifestyle. If that sum constituted your entire capital, it is doubtful whether the costs involved would justify the savings. Under current legislation you are allowed to remove £215,000 from this figure which would leave £285,000 subject to inheritance tax at 40 per cent which would amount to £84,000 payable to the Inland Revenue. The cost of whole of life assurance for that sum for someone aged 50 would be in the region of £840 per annum. This would eliminate the professional fees, set-up costs, possible CGT at the outset and continuing annual administrative charges.

WHAT TYPE OF POLICY IS THE MOST EFFECTIVE?

There are really only two basic types of policy which you should contemplate for the purpose of protecting your capital against the ravages of inheritance tax. They will be presented to you dressed up in many ways to make each one seem more attractive by way of benefits and cost savings, and frequently the extra charges will claim to have additional peripheral benefits attached to them. Since the sole objective from your point of view is to make provision for the any tax which may be payable, it is inadvisable to buy something which is festooned with unwanted bells and whistles, in my opinion. A basic policy which does the job and which costs the least to install is what is required. The two types of policy are as follows:

- term assurance
- whole of life

The only difference between the two is that one gives protection for a limited period, the other continues until death as long as the premiums are paid.

Term insurance

As the name says, such a policy will give you protection for a limited period which can be anything from a week to a number of years. I have known people take out term insurance to cover the risk to their capital from inheritance tax for a week when they had to fly to another territory for a business meeting and the estate which needed to be protected was of such magnitude that the cost of the short-term protection was irrelevant. Admittedly, the purpose of the visit was to arrange for the creation of an offshore trust with the objective of avoiding any liability to inheritance tax, so that such short term cover was put in place as an interim measure but this would not necessarily be something which most people would need to contemplate.

The normal arrangement would be for term insurance to cover a period of say, 20 years. Whilst this type of insurance is the cheapest, it does have one particular drawback. Suppose the age at the outset at which the life to be insured was 50 years old, and the term for the protection was taken out for 20 years. If the person whose life was the subject of the insurance died one day after their 70th birthday, there would be no cover at all and there would be no-pay out whatsoever. Now you may say that as the term was nearing its end, the obvious thing to do would be to extend the period of cover by taking out another policy for say, another ten or 15 years. This would be foolish because by the time the person concerned had reached the age of, say 68, the cost of a new term insurance would be prohibitive and might even exceed the amount which would be payable by way of tax anyway. So do not be persuaded that what appears now to be a relatively cheap form of protection will give you the best value for money for what is one of the most important parts of your financial planning.

Whole of life assurance

This type of policy provides cover from the moment that it has been underwritten and accepted until death occurs, provided that the premiums are paid. Unlike term insurance, which is for a limited period during which there may or may not be a claim against the underwriters, under this policy there will be a claim at some time in the future. Obviously the younger the life to be assured is at the time of the inception of the policy, the cheaper the annual cost of premiums. Nevertheless such costs can be onerous, particularly if the estate which will be the subject of the probate valuation consists largely of land or assets which have a high value but which do not generate sufficient surplus net income after the costs of repairs and mainte-nance. However this type of policy remains by far and away the most effective for the mitigation of inheritance tax. It will pay you to arrange for the policy cover to increase each year by the amount of inflation, particularly if you start it when you are rela-tively young. It will cost slightly more in premiums but the gain far outweighs the extra charge.

> '... do not be persuaded that what appears now to be a relatively cheap form of protection will give you the best value for money ...'

The policy can be taken out when both spouses are alive but with the proviso that any claim will only become payable on the death of the last survivor. Under such an arrangement it matters not which spouse dies first.

A TAX-EFFECTIVE WAY TO PAY THE PREMIUMS

There is a concession under current legislation which allows you to make annual gifts up to a total of £3,000 free of tax to the recipient. If you set up a whole of life assurance policy with inflation-proofing included, you can gift the amount of the annual premium to one of the beneficiaries so that he or she can pay the insurance company. Or alternatively, a beneficiary can instigate the policy in the first place with you making a gift each year of an amount equal to the cost of the premium. In either case, the proceeds of the policy would remain out-side your estate for probate purposes and consequently they would not attract inheritance tax. You would have to make sure that the funds payable by the insurance company were applied to the payment of any inheritance tax rather than being spent on something else.

SUMMARY

In this chapter we have looked at the following items:

- the use that life assurance can play in prudent tax planning if it is used properly;
- the way to calculate the amount of cover needed without incurring a large financial burden;
- the importance of writing any life assurance in trust;
- the dangers inherent in transferring assets off shore and the minimum size of an estate required before such a move is worthwhile financially.

GLOSSARY

Accounting period   The period of time, usually 12 months, over which the trading activities of a company are recorded. On the Stock Exchange it is the number of days, now usually one, over which bargains are executed.

Accounts   A summary of the records accumulated during the accounting period.

Advisory service   The service offered by stockbrokers or financial intermediaries where specific advice on investments may be given. See *Execution-only*.

Annual General Meeting (AGM)   A meeting for the shareholders of a company which must be held by law once each year. It must include certain items within the agenda for approval by the shareholders, including the acceptance of the company *Report & Accounts*, the election of directors, the permission to pay a dividend and the approval of the auditors' remuneration. Sometimes referred to as an 'Ordinary' meeting, it needs 21 clear days' notice to shareholders if it is to be legal. See *Statutory Notice*.

Asset Value   The current value of any assets underlying a share. See *Net Asset Value*.

Auditor   A qualified person, usually a chartered accountant, authorised to approve and sign company accounts.

Auditors' Reports   The reports signed by the company's auditors verifying that they have carried out the inspection of the accounts as required by law. See *Qualified Accounts*.

Authorised Capital   The sum of money which a company is authorised by its shareholders to seek subscription by way of the issuance of shares from the public and/or existing shareholders. See *Issued Capital*.

Balance Sheet   A statement of the current values of the assets and liabilities of a company and the value of the shareholders' funds. See *Report & Accounts*.

Bear   One who believes that the market is going to decline in value. See *Bull*.

Bear Market   The name given to the market which is declining in value, usually as a result of an excess of sellers over buyers. It can be attributed to an individual share also. See *Bull Market*.

Bid   The price which is offered by a market maker to the seller of a share. Also the price which one company offers to buy the shares of another company in a takeover situation.

Bid/Offer Spread   The difference in money between the price at which a market maker is prepared to buy a share from a seller and the price at which he will sell the same share to a buyer.

Blue Chip   A name given to a share of a company which is thought to be safer than most. See *Gilt*.

Bought Bargain   A purchase of a stock or share. See *Closing Bargain*.

Broker   An intermediary authorised by the Securities and Futures Authority (SFA) to negotiate buying and selling securities with the market makers on behalf of the public.

Broker Nominee Account   A single corporate register of ownership of shares in the name of the broker nominee company on the company register held by the broker on behalf of individual shareholders.

Bull   One who believes the market is going to go up in value. See *Bear*.

Bull Market   The name given to a market which is appreciating in value, usually because of an excess of buyers over sellers. It can be attributed to an individual share also. See *Bear Market*.

Buy In   The action that is taken by a market maker against the seller of a security if that security has not delivered the stock to the market within the specified time allowed.

Buy To Close   A purchase of an option or future to close a previously bought position.

Buy To Open   A purchase of an option or future to open up a holding.

Call   A sum of money which is payable for a share at a future date. See *Nil Paid*.

Call Option   The right to buy a share at or before a date in the future at a price agreed at the time of purchasing the call option. See *Put Option*.

Capital Gain   The amount of net profit after all costs between the purchase price and selling price of a security.

Capital Gains Tax   The tax levied on the annual amount of capital gain accumulated during the year 6 April to the following 5 April.

Chairman's Statement   The statement made to shareholders each year, which is included in the company *Report*, describing the opinion of the board of directors concerning the future expectations of the company's progress.

Chart   A graphic representation of numbers measured against a time scale. Usually a record of the performance of a share price over a period of time.

Closing Bargain   A sale of a bought bargain within the account period (usually the same day). See *Buy To Close*.

Closing Price   The price at which a share was quoted at the close of the market for the day. See *Mandatory Quote Period*.

Commission   The charge made by stockbrokers for executing bargains in the stock market. See *Consideration* and *Stamp Duty*.

Consideration   The amount of money payable or receivable for the purchase or sale of stocks or shares before charges. Consideration is calculated by multiplying the number of shares by the price at which they are bought or sold. See *Commission* and *Stamp Duty*.

Contract Note   A document confirming all the details of a purchase or sale, including the date of the bargain, the date on which settlement is due, name of the company, denomination of the share or stock, the number of shares or the amount of stock bought or sold, the price, commission, stamp duty (bought bargain only), charges, and net amount due for payment or receipt. It is an essential record and must be kept safely for production in the event of a contested claim in the future. See *Electronic Registration*.

Convertibles   A convertible share or loan stock is one where the shareholder has the right to convert the holding into ordinary shares at a date in the future. In the case of convertible shares, this right usually occurs for a period every year during the life of the share which may have a redemption date or be classified as irredeemable. Loan stock may be converted at a date in the future without requiring any permission from the stock holder, as is the case with gilts.

CREST   The electronic settlement system which has replaced the Talisman system.

Cum Dividend   The right of the owner of the share, before it is declared ex-dividend, to receive the next dividend due for payment.

Data   Factual information of any kind.

Database   A record of historic data, usually maintained in a computer.

Dealing   The negotiation and execution of purchases and sales.

Dealing Inside the Price   The execution of a purchase or sale at a price which is within the bid or offer price quoted on the dealing screens by the market maker. See *Touch*.

Designated Nominee Account   A stock or share holding within the broker's nominee account which carries a designation naming the individual holder which is recorded on the Company Register. See *Pooled Nominee Account*.

Discount   A price of an asset which is below the market value.

Dividend   A payment of money to the registered holder of a share by the company out of its earnings. See *Scrip Dividend*.

Dividend Cover   The number resulting from dividing the total amount to be paid out as dividend into the earnings of the company (pre-tax profits).

Earnings Per Share   The earnings (Pre-tax profits) of the company divided by the number of Ordinary shares in issue. See *Issued Capital*.

Electronic Registration   A system whereby a shareholding is recorded electronically on the share Register by the Registrar and where no paper share certificates are issued.

Ex-Dividend   The date from which a registered holder of the share or buyer of a share is not entitled to receive the next dividend payment. See *Cum Dividend*.

Execution Only   A broking service wherein the broker is forbidden to offer any advice but is confined to carrying out the instructions of the client to buy or sell a stock, share, future or option. See *Advisory Service*.

Extraordinary General Meeting   A meeting of shareholders to consider and vote on any proposal which is abnormal and outside the scope of an annual general meeting, e.g., to approve or reject a takeover proposal, or to alter the authorised or issued capital limits currently embodied in the *Memorandum & Articles of Association*. Notice of 28 clear days must be given to shareholders if such a meeting is to be legal. See *Annual General Meeting*.

Fixed-Interest Securities   Loans issued by a company, the government (gilts) or local authority, where the amount of interest to be paid each year is set at issue. Usually the date of repayment is also included in the title. See *Yield*.

FT-SE All Share   An index, published daily, of the weighted average of the mid-closing prices of all shares traded on the London Stock Exchange.

FTSE 100   An index of the weighted average of the middle prices of the shares of the top 100 companies measured by their market capitalisation.

FTSE 250   An index of the weighted average of the middle prices of the shares of the next 250 companies measured by their market capitalisation.

FTSE 350   An index of the weighted average of the middle prices of the shares of the next 350 companies measured by their market capitalisation.

Futures and Securities Authority (FSA)   The regulatory authority governing the conduct of all individuals and firms authorised to execute bargains on the London Stock Exchange and/or give advice to the public.

General PEP   A personal equity plan which is allowed to contain a mixture of investments in shares of different companies or shares and unit trusts or investment trusts. See *Personal Equity Plan*.

Gilt   The name given to loan stock issued by the Bank of England on behalf of the government. So called because the safety of the investment is said to be 'gilt-edged'. See *Blue Chip*.

Graph   Another name for a chart. See *Chart*.

Gross Dividend   The amount of the dividend payable on a share before the deduction of tax by the company. See *Net Dividend*.

Grossing Up   The factor by which the net dividend must be multiplied to discover the amount of the gross dividend.

High   The highest price which a stock or share or index has reached during a given period. See *Low*.

Index   A method of measuring the performance of a stock, share, future, option, sector, market, currency or commodity.

Indexation   The factor by which share holders are allowed to increase the purchase price of a stock or share (sometimes called re-basing) before calculating the gains to compensate for inflation. This concession can have a considerable effect in reducing any liability to capital gains tax if the investment has been held for several years. See *Capital Gains Tax*.

Interest   The annual payment made to the holder of loan stock or fixed interest securities such as Preference shares. The amount is expressed in percentage terms and is sometimes referred to as a coupon. See *Fixed-interest securities*.

Investing   Buying a stock or share, usually with the intention of holding it for some time. See *Trading*.

Investment Trust   A fund which is invested into shares which are listed and traded on a stock exchange and is managed by a fund manager. The management of the fund is governed by Trustee laws. The shares in the investment trust are themselves listed and traded on the market. The number of shares in issue are limited, similar to any PLC., and the investment trust company has the right to borrow money for investment purposes over and above the capital raised by issuing shares. See *Unit Trust*.

Issued Capital   The amount of money which is issued to the market by way of shares in the company. The amount of the issued capital must not exceed the amount of the authorised capital as defined in the company's *Memorandum and Articles of Association*. Any change will require approval from shareholders at an extraordinary general meeting.

Limit   The price of a share, above which a buyer is not prepared to buy, or, below which a seller is not prepared to sell.

Limit Order   An instruction to a broker to execute a bargain within a limit set by the client.

Loan Stock   Money borrowed from the public by way of the market, which is traded on the Stock Exchange, usually bearing a fixed amount of interest payable annually. Gilts are included in this category. Loan stock may or may not be secured on the underlying assets of the company. Secured loan stock is considered to be more secure in the event of the company being wound up. Loan stock may or may not be convertible into ordinary shares at a future date. See *Convertibles*.

Long-Term Investor   The description given to someone who buys stocks or shares with the intention of holding them for three years or more.

Low   The lowest price which a stock or share or index has reached during a given period. See *High*.

Mandatory Quote Period   The period between 0830 and 1630 every day whilst the market is open during which the market makers must exhibit bid and offer prices for the shares in which they make a market. See *Size*.

Market Capitalisation   The measurement of the size of a company which is achieved by multiplying the number of ordinary shares in issue by the current market price (usually the mid-closing price from the previous day).

Market Maker   A firm authorised to deal in stocks and shares on their own account by buying from and selling to the public or fund managers via an intermediary. Also authorised to make their own prices for stocks and shares and to change them at will.

Net Asset Value   The value of an asset after allowing for any charges or depreciation. It is a standard comparison against the share price of investment trusts.

Net Dividend   The amount of dividend receivable after the removal of tax by the company at the prevailing rate.

Nil Paid   A new share which is issued for no consideration, but where payment may be due in the future. These are usually rights issues and often they can be bought or sold in the market, but the buyer must pay the call when it becomes due.

Nominal Value   The nominal value, or denomination, is the value given to a share or loan stock at the time of issue. It need have no connection with the price which is paid for it. For instance, a 10p nominal ordinary share might have a current market price of 740p or any other figure. A gilt with a nominal value of 100 could be trading at 98.5 or 119.25.

Normal Market Size (NMS) This is the maximum number of shares to which the screen quotation made by a market maker applies for both buying and selling. The amounts may vary in either case. A requirement to deal in larger quantities than the NMS may be possible, but the market maker is not bound by the quotation for any part of a deal outside the NMS.

Offer The price at which a market maker is prepared to sell a share to a buyer. See *Bid*.

Ordinary Share Often called equity, the ordinary share is the normal instrument representing the issued capital of a company and it carries the most risk. For example, the issued capital might be £1,000,000 divided into 10 million ordinary shares of 10p each. Unless a share is described differently, e.g., Preference or Convertible.

Personal Equity Plan (PEP) A fund which is permitted to hold investments in most classes of shares or unit trusts and investment trusts and which is not transferable but belongs to the individual. All capital gains and any income arising out of the investments is free from income tax and capital gains tax. A personal equity plan can be created for each financial year. See *Single Company PEP*.

Pooled Nominee Account An account within the broker's nominee company wherein all the shares owned by clients in one company are registered on the Company Register under the name of the nominee company and appear on the Register as one holding. See *Designated Nominee Account*.

Pre-Tax Profit The profit which a company makes after all charges but before tax.

Preference Share A share in a company which takes preference over the ordinary shares both for the payment of dividends and in the distribution of the assets in the event of the company being wound up.

Premium The amount by which the market value of a share or stock exceeds the current underlying value of the share or stock. See *Discount*.

Price Earnings Ratio   The current share price divided by the last published earnings per share. See *Earnings Per Share*.

Profit and Loss Account   Part of the published accounts of a company which are subject to the auditors report and must be signed by the auditor.

Qualified Accounts   Accounts for the company which fail to satisfy the inspection of the auditor. An investor should beware of any accounts which are qualified. Any qualification must be published in the annual *Report and Accounts* which is always available from the Company Secretary.

Re-Basing   An adjustment to the purchase price of a share to allow for the effects of inflation.

Registrar   A person or company authorised to maintain the list of current shareholders for a company including their names and addresses and the quantity of shares held in each name. Registrars also issue dividend payments and tax vouchers to shareholders who qualify for dividends. Some companies employ their own in-house registrar.

Regulatory Authority   An authority with powers to regulate the conduct of members and firms who operate in the securities industry with particular regard for the safe guarding of the interests of the investing public. Part of their duty is to investigate complaints from investors and they have the ability to remove operating licences from any member or firm who, in their opinion, has acted with impropriety or been found to be guilty of misconduct either in giving advice or from managing investors' funds.

Report and Accounts   The official statements showing the assets and liabilities of a company together with details of all income and expenses including wages and salaries. They must be produced once a year by law and they must be audited. See *Auditor* and *Qualified Accounts*.

Reserves   Money which a company has earned which is set aside to be used in the management of the company if unforeseen situations occur in the future which require funding.

Resistance Level   A share price level from which the price is likely to rebound in a downward direction. This is usually established by projecting historic share price performance forwards and is useful in forecasting probable share price behaviour. See *Support Level*.

Retail Price Index (RPI) An index which is published around the 15 of each month showing the factor by which inflation has risen or fallen. It applies to the penultimate month, because it takes time to collate all the data, e.g., the RPI figure for February will be published in April.

Return On Capital Employed A figure which shows how efficient or otherwise the management of a company is in operating the company each year. It is obtained by dividing the trading profit by the shareholders' funds and multiplying by 100. It is expressed as a percentage and its value is for comparison with similar calculations for the preceding years.

Rolling Settlement A system which has replaced the old stock exchange account period and which requires all bargains executed on a day to be settled by a set day in the future. If a purchase is made on Day 1 for settlement on Day 5, and a sale is made on Day 2 for settlement on Day 6, the client must pay for the purchase on Day 5 even though he or she will be expecting to receive the proceeds of the sale on Day 6. See *Settlement Date*.

Settlement Date The date on which payment must be made for purchases and payment is received for sales. It may be possible to arrange for the proceeds of a sale made subsequent to a purchase on a prior date to be set against the cost of the purchase but any such arrangement must be entered into at the time of the sale and agreed before the bargain is executed.

Share Certificate A certificate which proclaims ownership of a quantity of shares in a given company. They are issued by the Registrar. If share certificates are held by an investor, as opposed to electronic registration, the time required for settlement of a sale will be longer and there will probably be extra charges incurred as a result. See *Electronic Registration*.

Share Register The list of owners of shares in a company showing their names, addresses and quantity held at any time.

Share Shop An address made available to the public which belongs to an authorised firm dealing in stocks and shares wherein buyers and sellers may give instructions to deal in securities. Usually screens are available giving real-time share prices.

Shareholders' Funds An item shown on the balance sheet of a company's report and accounts representing surplus and undesignated money which, at the time when the accounts were drawn up, belong to the shareholders.

Short-Term Trader   Someone who expects to buy a share or place a spread bet and achieve a profit within a short period of time.

Single Company PEP   A personal equity plan wherein the shares of one company only are purchased. Under current legislation the maximum amount of £3,000 must be subscribed into a single company PEP at the outset, and a new one can be set up each financial year. The new one can be invested in the shares of a different company but the sum of money to be invested remains the same.

Size   The number of shares to be bought or sold within the order, e.g., an investor may want to sell 150,000 shares in one company and that would be called the size of the order. However, if there were only two market makers for the share and the prices which they were quoting were in sizes of 10,000 shares, there could well be a problem in disposal of the holding at the current market price.

Sponsored Membership   A method of identifying an individual share holding on the share register when shares are electronically registered.

Stamp Duty   An impost demanded by the government on every purchase of stocks or shares amounting currently to 0.5 per cent of the purchase consideration. There is no stamp duty levied at present on sales.

Statutory Notice   The number of clear days which must elapse between publishing notice of a meeting of shareholders and the meeting taking place. An annual general meeting (or ordinary meeting) requires 21 clear days, an extraordinary meeting requires 28 clear days. See *Annual General Meeting* and *Extraordinary Meeting*.

Stop-Loss   The price level at which a shareholder instructs the broker to sell the holding to minimise a capital loss or lock in a gain.

Support Level   A line drawn on a chart indicating a share price level from which it is expected the share price will bounce in an upward direction. See *Resistance Level*.

Touch   The highest bid price and the lowest offer price available at any moment from all the market makers' prices quoted on the dealing screen. The two prices may well be taken from different market makers, and usually this is the case. See *Dealing Inside the Price*.

Trading   Buying and selling stocks and shares.

Trading Range   Parallel lines drawn on a chart separated by the highs and lows of a share price over a recent period of time.

Transfer Form   A document which the seller of a security has to sign transferring ownership of the security to someone else.

Trend   The direction, which is easily seen on a chart, of the progress of a share price over a specific period of time.

Unit Trust   A portfolio of holdings in various companies, divided into units and managed by professional fund managers. The number of units which may be issued is unlimited and this is the fundamental difference between unit and investment trusts. A unit trust is not allowed to borrow money for investment. See *Investment Trusts*.

Volatility   The degree to which a share price rises and falls over a time period. Also called 'oscillation'.

Year End   The date on which a company draws up its accounts for audit purposes every year. Normally a 12-month period, except occasionally at the company's inception the period may cover more or less than 12 months. Sometimes, perhaps as a result of an acquisition or merger, the year-end date may be altered, but usually by not more than one month.

Yield   The amount of the annual return by way of dividend or interest on the cost of purchase of an individual stock or share at current market price expressed as a percentage. It is calculated by dividing the gross annual dividend or interest by the current mid-price and multiplying by 100. See *Grossing Up*, *Dividend* and *Interest*.

INDEX